THE ART OF THE JUGGLING ACT

The Art of the Juggling Act
Bite-Sized Guide for Working Parents

For information about this title or to order other books and/or electronic media, contact the publisher:

Life Journey Experiences, LLC
lifejourneyexperiences.com
thejugglingact.com

ISBNs:
978-0-9975613-2-6 (softcover)
978-0-9975613-3-3 (eBook)

LCCN: 2024910201

1106 Design in collaboration with Sarah Armstrong

Photo: Bess Friday Photography
Sculpture: Jon Krawczyk

THE ART OF THE JUGGLING ACT

BITE-SIZED GUIDE FOR WORKING PARENTS

SARAH ARMSTRONG

One of my goals in life is to show that

you can have a family and a career,

be happy in both aspects of your life,

and enjoy each day to the fullest.

It is a day-to-day juggling act.

However, if you enjoy what you do in both worlds,

then the juggling act is worth it.

TRIBUTES

This book is dedicated to...

Grace - My daughter, who is my inspiration to be the best Mom possible. Thank you for always understanding that I loved being your Mom and that I also loved working... and thank you for never making me feel guilty about trying to do both.

Dad - For being an amazing role model throughout my life in terms of always being there for your family and also showing how to lead a successful career with integrity, humility, and hard work.

Mom - For being an exceptional role model by putting your family first and showing the importance of traditions, creating a welcoming home to entertain your family and friends, as well as for showing the importance of giving back to your community.

My Working-Mom Friends - Thank you for always being there to compare notes and support each other as we were each managing our own juggling act. It is a gift I will never forget.

My Stay-at-Home Mom Friends - Thank you for always being there when I needed you... never making me feel guilty for asking for help... and never judging what I was trying to juggle.

PREFACE

When I was six years old, I have a memory of going to my dad's office (he was a hospital CEO)... I remember sitting at his desk and saying to myself, "Someday, I want to run something."

I was not one of those children who knew what I wanted to be when I grew up. However, what I did know is that I wanted to have a career and a family. This part of the vision for my life was always clear to me.

From a career standpoint, I have always enjoyed my various roles which has been rewarding. In the following section, I share a bit about my career path, and, if you want more details, please see my bio at the end of the book.

I have one daughter, Grace, and I am proud to say her wings are spread and that she is taking flight out in the world.

Over the years, I have been asked by younger colleagues for advice on various aspects of managing a career and a family. There was a phase in my career where I was managing a team of all young working moms. We had countless discussions about the various aspects of juggling work and family. After many of these discussions, my team members would tell me that I should really write all of this guidance down. However, I did not consider myself a writer and did not think I would ever actually take the time to write a book on this topic.

It was when I wrote a book after my divorce called *The Mom's Guide to a Good Divorce* that I learned how fulfilling it was to share my advice with women who are trying to figure things out. Once I finished my first book, it gave me the understanding and the confidence in terms of what it would take to write this book.

The purpose of this book is to help individuals who are thinking about what it will take to have a career and a family or who are already in the midst of the day-to-day juggling act required to manage a career and a family. Either way, my goal in writing this book is to share guidance from my journey as well as from other working women who are my close friends. These women have had various career paths within marketing, legal, medicine, management consulting, sales, and entrepreneurial endeavors. They have been on their own journeys to figure out how to manage all of the aspects of their lives, while still keeping a sense of humor and their sanity (which is not always a given).

Throughout this book, there are points covered which are specific to a certain socio-economic situation. Please feel free to skip over these points if they are not relevant to you. However, the vast majority of the guidance in this book should be helpful as you navigate the day-to-day of being a working parent.

Hopefully, after reading this book, you will come away with a few nuggets of wisdom to reflect upon and to apply to your own juggling act. I should highlight that each of our juggling acts are unique in their own special way... whether you are married or a single working parent... whether your spouse/ partner works or stays at home... whether you have family around you to provide support or you rely on a nanny or daycare for help... or you just try to juggle everything solo. I hope you will find my guidance useful, whether you work full-time or part-time, whether you work in an office, work from home, or work in a hybrid model... and whether you travel for your job or primarily stay in town.

Regardless of your specific scenario, I am hoping you will find both understanding and comfort that you are not alone in trying to figure out how to juggle. It is an ever-evolving landscape that you are trying to manage, depending on the ages of your children as well as what stage you are in from a career standpoint... and the other dynamics you are managing in your personal life.

MY JUGGLING ACT

After graduating from Georgetown with a degree in Marketing, I decided to move to Chicago and join Leo Burnett (which is an advertising agency). This was a fun way to start my career in an amazing city. I worked hard (and very long hours) in those early years, but I learned a lot about working in an agency and about Marketing.

During these years, I was fortunate to work for a very special woman, Renetta McCann, at Leo Burnett. She was a working mom with two young children. She was one of the first women I was able to work with who was managing the juggling act. Renetta was a true inspiration to me and showed that it was possible to have a family and a successful career.

Then, I moved to Atlanta with my fiancé and joined The Coca-Cola Company in Global Marketing. This was the start of my globetrotting, which changed my life forever. I loved working with people from various cultures around the world. With each trip to another country and the special people that I had the opportunity to work with, I grew as a person and truly became a citizen of the world.

When I was thirty years old, I had Grace, and this is when my juggling act began. I was in a global role at The Coca-Cola Company and still doing significant international travel as part of my role (basically had a week-long international trip once a month). My husband traveled domestically each week, so we had a nanny who would stay with Grace during the weeks when both of us were gone.

My career continued to progress over the years, with more leadership responsibility. Along with the evolution in responsibilities, I continued thinking through how I was going to manage the juggling act and refine my working-mom operating model each year.

When Grace was seven years old, I went through a divorce, and this required me to evaluate all aspects of my juggling act. I needed to ensure that I could continue to do all that I was trying to do in both my personal life and my professional life... and I was committed to figuring it out.

When Grace was in eighth grade, I left The Coca-Cola Company and decided to join McKinsey & Company as a Partner. This required even more travel than I was doing before (on a weekly basis)... and further refinement of how I was managing the juggling act.

During Grace's junior year in high school, I left McKinsey to join Google to lead Global Marketing Operations. This was during the pandemic, so I had the opportunity to work from home and have lots of quality time with Grace in her final two years at home. This time together was truly a gift.

This was also the first time that Grace had really seen me "work," because I had always gone to an office (and did not work at home when I was with her). The silver lining of the pandemic is that Grace gained an appreciation for how invested I was in what I did each day... and how much I enjoyed my work.

Over the years of raising Grace, I constantly evaluated how I was doing in managing the juggling act... always keeping her as the priority... and took it on as a challenge to figure out how to make it all work. As I look back, I am proud of how I approached my juggling act... it was not easy, but it was definitely worth it.

PAYING IT FORWARD

One of the reasons that I felt compelled to write this book is the fulfillment it gives me to pay it forward to other working parents who are trying to figure out how to manage the juggling act on a day-to-day basis.

I will never claim to have all of the answers for how to approach being a working parent... but I have spent the past twenty-one years focused on figuring out how to make all aspects of my life work to the best of my ability and enjoy life each day.

Over the years, many of my younger colleagues have asked me for guidance as they are thinking through the dynamics of the juggling act. I hope this book plays a part in helping the next generation of working parents reflect on how to juggle and live life to the fullest.

Now let's talk a bit about juggling...

JUGGLING FIVE BALLS

This is a quote that I always had hanging on the wall in my office as a reminder to myself...

"Imagine life as a game in which you are juggling five balls in the air.

You name them...
work, family, friends, health, and spirit...
and you're keeping all of these in the air.

You will soon understand that work is a rubber ball.

If you drop it, it will bounce back.

But the other four balls...
family, friends, health, and spirit... are made of glass.

If you drop one of these, they will be irreparably scuffed, marked, nicked, damaged, or even shattered."

James Patterson

I have added a reflection to this quote...

"The glass balls will never be the same.
You must understand this and strive for balance in your life that works for you as you manage the juggling act."

NOTE: A fun point to share is that I designed the sculpture on the front cover to reflect this quote and the five balls we juggle in life... work, family, friends, health, and spirit. Then, I worked with a metal sculptor to create the sculpture. It now lives in my living room and makes me smile each time that I look at it.

THE GUIDE

There are so many different ways that families are structured these days, from a family that has a mom and a dad, two dads, two moms, a mom or a dad. However you define family, I hope this guide can be helpful to you.

This is the guide which would have been helpful for me to have to refer to when I was raising Grace, from both an emotional and practical standpoint. So, I have structured "The Guide" in specific buckets of topics. The reason this should be useful is that you can read a section at a time, absorb and process what you have read, and then set the book aside if you need to until you are ready to read the next section.

There is so much to think through when you are managing the juggling act. After discussing these details with my friends, I came to realize that there are no magic answers for managing your juggling act... and you figure it out along the way.

It can be overwhelming to see all of the points that you need to think through listed out. Recognize that this is a journey you are on to raise your children, so take it in bite-sized pieces that you can handle as you manage your own juggling act each day.

Also, I want to highlight that what I am sharing with you is what I have learned over eighteen years of raising Grace and defining the traditions, routines, and learnings along the way as a working parent (as well as insights from my working-mom friends who have also already raised their children). So, if you are a new working parent, please do not feel that you have to have all of this figured out right away. This guide is just meant to share the range of things that you can think about as you are on your own journey.

A quick note about any reference to "working moms" versus "working parents" in this book. When I started writing this book, I was writing it from the perspective of being a working mom and the many discussions I had with other working moms over the years regarding the juggling act.

However, I now have numerous friends with different family structures and want to acknowledge that there are many working parents out in the world who are trying to manage the juggling act, so the guidance I want to share is meant for all working parents. There may be instances where you see a reference to "working moms," and this was a conscious call-out from my perspective, given the point I am trying to share on a given topic.

Hopefully, this can be a guide you can refer to as you navigate your juggling act over the years.

BITE-SIZED PIECES

A short note about the design of this book... it has been written specifically for the mindset of an individual who is starting to think through what it will take to raise children and manage a career... or who is already in the midst of juggling family and career.

So, I have decided to put only one topic on a page and have included as much white space as possible to provide space for you to think about the specific topic.

Turn the page only when you are ready for the next topic... that could be tomorrow, next week, or next month.

CONTENTS

SO... WHERE TO BEGIN?

MINDSET IS ESSENTIAL

The mindset that you enter into as a working parent is essential to understand. There are some of us who have always wanted to work and have a family. There are some of us who would prefer to stay home with our children, but, due to financial considerations, we have to work. There are some of us who work part-time, and there are some of us who work full-time.

Whatever scenario you are in, the mindset you use to approach your situation will define how your children, your family, your friends, and your colleagues view how you are approaching your life. This is not to say that you should try to be positive for the sake of being positive. It is to say that if you are in a position where the juggling act is your reality, you need to figure out the mindset that will help you to manage the juggling act in the healthiest way possible to enjoy your day-to-day life.

Just remember that you will create your own version of the juggling act. Do what works for you, and don't compare yourself to colleagues and friends... everyone's juggling act is going to be different.

DESIGNING YOUR LIFE

When you think about the life you want to lead, there are choices we all make...

- ~ Where do you want to live?

- ~ How do you want to live?

- ~ What type of work do you want to do?

- ~ Where do you want to work?

- ~ Who do you want to spend your time with... spouse/partner, family and friends?

- ~ What experiences do you want to have?

At some point, you may decide to have children, and then there is the choice of how you want to structure your life with children... whether you work full-time or part-time, or stay at home.

Obviously, two of those choices are dependent on the financial situation you are in at the time and whether it is viable to work part-time or to stay at home.

However, I do believe that we all have the power to choose the life we want to lead and then think through how we want to design and structure our lives to be as happy as possible, given the choices we have made along the way.

THE CONCEPT OF "HAVING IT ALL"

Our society has put pressure on women to try to "have it all." When I reflect on this concept, I think it is all relative to what you want out of life. "Having it all" looks very different to different women. So, my recommendation is to define for yourself what "having it all" means and strive for that vision. The vision you have for your life is all that really matters. What society has said your life should look like is not important.

There is also the pressure of comparing our own lives to what others post on social media about their lives. It may look like everyone is "having it all" because they generally post only the positive highlights. We all know that all of our day-to-day lives have positive and challenging moments... that is the reality of life. So, don't spend time comparing yourself to others and trying to live up to a societal benchmark. Just focus on what you want out of life, and define what "having it all" means to you.

THE DEFINITION OF BALANCE

The word "balance" is used a lot when discussing how we approach life. When we attempt the juggling act, there is a lot of talk about balance. The thing about balance is that it can mean different things to different people, depending on what you are capable of managing in your life.

I have found that my definition of "balance" is atypical, but it works for me, and that is all that really matters.

For example, over the years, I needed to work some evenings during the week due to the role I have played, but this does not mean I am not balanced. I have figured out a definition of "balance" that is unique to my life, what my family needed at different stages along the way, and what fit with the lifestyle I wanted to lead as a working mom.

I am one who likes to fit as much into my day as possible. I have so much I want to accomplish in life, so, for me, balance means that I am able to accomplish all that I want to accomplish in a given day or week from a personal and professional standpoint.

There are definitely times when I have been out of balance and was not giving enough time to my personal life, especially early on in my career. I learned over time what the right level of "balance" was for my life. There were times when I felt that all I was doing was working and taking care of Grace, and that everything else in my life was not getting the attention it deserved (e.g., my health, my friends, etc.). In the moments when I realized this was the case, I needed to try to make some shifts in how I was approaching things (see next section).

So, figure out what your definition of "balance" is, and then think through how your day-to-day operating model (which I will cover in a later section) can help you achieve the balance you are striving for.

It may seem like you do not have the time or space to figure out your definition of "balance." The reality is that you are trying to balance each day within your own juggling act. So, if you can, take the time to briefly reflect on what is/is not working well for you on any given day, week, or month... and ask yourself how you are feeling about how you are currently balancing the various aspects of your life. This is how you eventually will figure out your own definition of "balance" that works for your life.

Remember that your definition of "balance" may evolve over time, and that is okay... that is what this juggling act is all about.

ALLOWING FOR TIMES OF IMBALANCE

Throughout our lives, there are times when we feel completely out of balance. This is definitely going to occur... it is just a matter of when, as our feeling of work/life balance ebbs and flows.

So, when this feeling of "imbalance" hits, try to think through what would help you get re-balanced. Is it a change in your routines at home and/or at work? Is it a change in the support you need to have in place at home? Is it the decisions you are making to prioritize everyone else... over yourself?

Whatever the reason, try to identify what is causing the imbalance you are experiencing, and think about how you can try to change the dynamic. Generally, shifting an imbalance takes conscious effort. There are times when you inadvertently slip into habits that may be best for one part of your life but lead to you feeling out of balance in another part of your life.

The key thing to remember when imbalance occurs in your life is that it does not need to stay that way... you can work to reset dynamics in your life that are causing the imbalance. However, sometimes this is easier said than done, and there are trade-offs which need to be made for you to regain the balance you are striving for in your day-to-day life.

THE FEELING OF GUILT

One of the gifts that you can give to yourself is trying to minimize the feeling of guilt that many working parents have about the fact that they are not with their children all the time.

For some parents who work, it is a choice, because their financial situation does not depend on their income. However, for many, it is not a choice. So, we need to stop beating ourselves up about the fact that we are trying to juggle raising children while also managing a career.

Over the years, I have heard from various working moms that working is stimulating in a way that staying at home full-time is not (for certain women). What can help working moms with the guilt is the knowledge that, by working, we are exposing our children to a fuller, happier, more multi-dimensional version of ourselves, which is good for them to see. It also helps us to appreciate the time we do have with our children.

If you struggle with feelings of guilt, try to find others you can discuss these feelings with, whether it is friends who are working parents or a therapist.

Just try to remind yourself that you are doing the best you can, and really try to minimize those feelings of guilt.

PERFECTION IS NOT THE GOAL

This may sound trite, but it is true on so many levels. For many of us, there is still that niggling feeling that we should be striving for perfection at home and at work. We need to let this expectation go, as it will literally run us into the ground.

Try to give yourself the grace to know that you are doing the best you can, and take the pressure off yourself to strive for perfection. There is nothing in life that is perfect. The sooner we realize that we are just trying to juggle so much in our day-to-day, the sooner we can enjoy the journey and make peace with what we did not accomplish or do perfectly well. Then, we can focus on what is most important on any given day... raising our children and doing what we need to do at work.

There were many times throughout Grace's childhood that I would say to her, "Mom is doing the best she can." This was my way of acknowledging that I may not be doing things right, but that I was trying. It is no different from when we tell our children that we want them to just "do their best." We are going to make mistakes as parents... that is a given.

Just realize that you will not be perfect. No one is, but, generally speaking, the imperfections will not matter to anyone except you. There is no formula to getting this right... just the one that is right for you.

Remind yourself along the way that we are all works in progress, and that is always the case.

BEING FLEXIBLE IS THE PLAN

Flexibility is key to being a working parent because you have to be ready to quickly deviate from the plan you had for any given day or week. Your children might get sick and need to go to a last-minute doctor appointment. They might forget an important item, and you need to drop it off at school. Inevitably, their sports practice/event will be rained out.

When Grace was in pre-school, I received a call that she had fallen on the playground and had an area under her chin that appeared to require stitches. I was in the middle of a meeting at work and excused myself to go and get Grace and take her to the emergency room to get stitched up. It is in these moments that we are reminded of what is most important... and that is to be there for our children.

There is always something that comes up... even during the most well-planned week... which requires you to use your flexibility muscle. This means that, during any given week, "good enough" should be the expectation. As I mentioned earlier, there were many days I would tell myself... "You are doing the best that you can... and that is good enough."

FIND LEVITY IN THE MISHAPS

There are inevitably times in life when things go wrong... whether it is getting a flat tire on the way to school while driving carpool, or a pipe bursting in your basement and you have to juggle dealing with your children while trying to figure out what to do with the water damage (my real-life examples).

When these mishaps in life occur, do what you can to try to find a moment of levity to just laugh at whatever happened and know that it was beyond your control.

Being able to laugh in these moments can help the situation and help your children to see how to roll with these situations when they come up in life.

TAKE TIME TO REFLECT

As I started each new year, I would try to set aside some time on New Year's Day to reflect on my goals for the year (and how I did on achieving my goals from the prior year). Many of these goals had to do with thinking through how I was going to fit everything in that I wanted to do in my day-to-day life.

Some years, my goals were quite simple... read more books or listen to more podcasts that teach me something new.

Other years, the goals were more complex... for example, when I went through a divorce and needed to figure out how to operate as a single working mom.

However, regardless of the year, there was always a moment where I would step back and try to give myself credit for managing the juggling act. Some years, I handled this better than others but managed it nonetheless.

These are important moments for us as parents because there are very few moments in life (beyond Mother's Day and Father's Day) when we receive recognition for all that we are trying to do to help raise our family, maintain our household, and also manage our career.

STRENGTHENING YOUR JUGGLING MUSCLE

Throughout our lives, we build many muscles, and one of the muscles we generally build is the ability to juggle the many things in life that we want to be involved in on a daily basis.

For the children who are currently growing up, this muscle is potentially built at an even earlier age than it was for their parents, due to the expectation of being involved in so many activities as a child, teen, and young adult.

Regardless of the age that you developed your own juggling muscle growing up, it can be tested as you become a working parent. This is because what you are juggling in raising your children and, at the same time, delivering on expectations at work are both significant demands and require a great deal of attention to do them both well.

It is fair to say that you can strengthen your juggling muscle, but it does take conscious effort to think through what you want to strengthen and the impact that will have on your day-to-day juggling act.

Hopefully the guidance in this book can help you as you are working on strengthening your juggling muscle.

TAKE A MOMENT
TO REFLECT...

WORKING PARENT OPERATING MODEL

The "Working Parent Operating Model" is a constant work in progress throughout the years that you raise your children. It changes every year based on the age of your children and what they need... at the same time, you have to factor in the demands at work and the other demands in your personal life.

When I refer to the "operating model," I mean how you structure your life to manage both your family and your career in a healthy and sustainable manner.

The details of your operating model include the support system you have in place to help with your children, the resources you put in place to help with things at home, and the boundaries you set at work to ensure you can manage both of your worlds as you need to.

There are times when you will want to pause and think through the approach you are taking to raising your children and managing your career, and I always ask myself these questions...

~ When are you the best parent?

~ When are you the best at work?

As I reflected on the answers to these questions, it helped me to continue to hone my operating model over the years.

Also, as you continue to refine and evolve your operating model, look for role models you can talk to, and ask them what they did to make it work. Every individual in the midst of managing the juggling act will have tips about what works for them that you can learn from and potentially apply in your life.

DIFFERENT TYPES OF PARENTS

When you think about the different types of parents in the world, there is a spectrum... there are stay-at-home parents and working parents. There are married working parents and single working parents. There are working parents who are always in town, and there are those working parents who travel.

Over the years, I have reflected on a certain dynamic that can take place between stay-at-home moms and working moms. The dynamic I am going to articulate does not always exist, but it is persistent enough to reflect upon as you may experience this as a working mom.

Based on my experience over the years, there are two types of stay-at-home moms... those who will judge the fact that you have not chosen to stay at home and raise your children, and those who admire what you are trying to do in terms of juggling a career and a family and are there to support you along the way.

Over the years, I could identify both types of stay-at-home moms a mile away. It clearly defined who I would engage with and who I decided would not be healthy for me to engage with beyond interactions at school or running into them around town.

The first interaction that has stuck with me over the years is when I went to drop Grace off at pre-school, and I was dressed in my pantsuit (back in the day when that is what you wore to work). A mom approached me, dressed in a tennis outfit, and said, "So, you are Grace's mom?" I answered that I was. She said, "Do you really travel internationally for your job?" I said, "Yes, I leave Grace with her father and our nanny." She gave me a look of what I can only describe as disdain and judgment and walked off without saying another word.

On the flip side, I have a number of very close girlfriends who are stay-at-home moms who have been very supportive of me and my career and have always offered to be there if we needed anything.

One of my girlfriends reflected that there are various mind-sets that you can run into... those who really think children should be the total focus of at least one parent, and those who wish they were you. There are those who work and beat themselves up about it, and there are those who stay home wishing they could figure out how to get back to work. There is no perfect answer.

At the end of the day, it is important to embrace the fact that you are a working parent and that you just need to be the best working parent you can be.

SINGLE WORKING PARENTS

If you are a single working parent versus a married working parent, there is definitely a different support structure needed in place when you are a single working parent.

The reality is that single working parents generally will have a much more challenging time with the juggling act than married working parents, as you are trying to manage everything by yourself.

From my standpoint, I have been both types of working parent in my career, as I was both married and divorced over the years that I raised Grace. However, I also had the fortunate situation of having an ex-husband who wanted to be actively involved in co-parenting Grace with me. So, we shared various responsibilities across two households.

The important thing to remember as a single working parent is that you are going to need help. It is a matter of defining how you structure this help to manage all that you need to manage each day. Throughout this book, I will cover a range of topics you will need to think through in terms of putting the right support system in place to help manage the juggling act.

NOTE: For more guidance on being a single working parent post-divorce, please see my book *The Mom's Guide to a Good Divorce*, which is a practical guide for everything you need to think through when you are going through a divorce and children are involved. This book includes specific guidance on how to partner with your ex-spouse/partner to co-parent your children in a healthy manner.

TRAVELING WORKING PARENTS

There is a difference between a working parent who does not need to travel for their jobs and those who travel often (and some who travel every week).

The range of dynamics that you need to manage when you are a traveling working parent requires you to be incredibly organized as you prepare to leave your children with the other parent, a nanny, a family member, or a friend.

The "pre-wiring," as I refer to it, which needs to happen when you are preparing for a trip, will ensure that all of the details that need to be handled for your children have been thought about in advance. Those who are watching your children should also be clear on these details.

Even when you have all of the details handled, there is always something that may come up while you are out of town.

There was an instance when Grace was in grade school, and I was traveling to London. The school called to let me know that I needed to pick Grace up because the school had to close due to a pipe bursting. Needless to say, I let the school know that I would not be able to pick her up but that Grace's nanny would be there soon to do so.

These are the moments when you will need to rely on those individuals whom you have selected to care for your children to handle these details, because there is a good chance you are not going to be able to help (in any meaningful way), given that you are out of town.

DIFFERENT TYPES OF SPOUSE/PARTNER

When you make the decision to be a working parent, you may or may not know if your spouse/partner will be there to co-parent with you and run the house with you as you had envisioned.

In some instances, you may be clear that you have a spouse/partner who will be there with you every step of the way to divide up responsibilities. In other instances, you may be entering into a "trial and error" phase as you see how things pan out.

It is sometimes hard to predict how our spouse/partner will react to the juggling act you have collectively decided to enter into until you are in the midst of it. Then, you will learn whether or not your spouse/partner is up to it.

There are also different types of spouses and partners. There are those who want to be involved in the day-to-day of co-parenting and running the house with you. There are those who want to have a more traditional approach, where they work, and you juggle your career, raising the children, and running the house (needless to say, this is not an ideal model). There are those who decide they want to stay home and have you be the primary breadwinner for the family.

From all that I have observed, the juggling act is challenging regardless of the support of your spouse/partner, but it becomes increasingly more challenging the more you are expected to do.

If you are in a situation where the division of labor is out of balance, then you need to think about whether you want to have a discussion with your spouse/partner to "renegotiate" the division of labor, or you may need to talk about bringing in extra help to clean, run errands, etc.

This can be a touchy subject to raise with your spouse/partner. However, if you are feeling that everything is falling on your shoulders, then you need to figure out how to raise the issue and think through the best approach to address the needs of your family. If you don't raise it, then there is a good chance you will start to resent your spouse/partner, and these negative feelings are not healthy to have in a relationship on an ongoing basis.

DUAL CAREER HOUSEHOLDS

If you and your spouse/partner both work, then there is definitely a need to discuss how you are going to jointly raise your children, run the household, and manage the logistics of life on a day-to-day basis.

For some couples, there is a natural dividing up of what needs to be done... and it all just works.

For many couples, there is a need to define the approach that will make the most sense, given the demands of each of your respective jobs and the travel requirements that may come with your roles.

Take the time to outline the various things that need to be done, and discuss with your spouse/partner who will take the lead on each element. There will be phases where one of you takes on more of the responsibility than the other. Try to avoid "keeping score" in terms of who is doing more during any given day, week, or month.

It may make sense to set aside time three to four times a year to reflect on what is working well with how you two are managing things and where there are potential opportunities to have things work better.

By the way, the demands of each of your roles may shift throughout the year, so there is a need for flexibility in terms of what has been agreed to between the two of you. This may sound straightforward, and you might be thinking, "Of course, we will do this," but given how busy our days can become, this type of discussion may not get the focus it deserves unless you consciously set aside time to discuss and work through things together.

SETTING & PROTECTING YOUR BOUNDARIES

The concept of setting boundaries can seem straightforward when you think about it. There are time-based boundaries, physical boundaries, and mental boundaries.

As a working parent, you need to create all three types of boundaries to help manage the day-to-day.

Reflect on what you want your boundaries to be and how to clearly define them for yourself. The reality is that, if you do not draw boundaries for yourself, then no one will. If you don't clearly define and communicate your boundaries to those who need to know, then they won't be able to respect them.

This applies to those you work with (e.g., manager and peers), those who may work for you (e.g., team or nanny), those you live with (e.g., spouse/partner or children), and those you interact with (e.g., friends). Everyone in your day-to-day ecosystem should understand the boundaries that you are trying to establish and maintain. Most people will respect your boundaries if they are aware of them. However, if you have not told anyone about your boundaries, then it is very hard for others to respect and honor the boundaries you have set for yourself.

PROTECTING YOUR TIME

As the saying goes, our time is precious. When you are a working parent, you never feel like you have enough time for whatever it is you are focused on in your personal or professional life.

So, one of the things that is important to do when you are trying to manage raising your children and your career is to protect the time you have set aside for whatever it is you are meant to be focused on.

This starts with setting time-based boundaries that help you protect your time. There are a couple of scenarios where this applies.

The first priority is to determine what you want your working hours to be and what you want your family hours to be (in an ideal situation). This will vary, depending on the type of role you are in and the demands of your job. However, thinking through the ideal situation helps you to define what you want to have as a daily schedule. Also, this schedule will shift as your children grow and are in different stages of life. So, you will be revisiting "the ideal" every couple of years (at a minimum).

When Grace was young (newborn to age six), I wanted to be able to spend some time in the morning together before I headed to work and also some evening time with her before bed. Practically speaking, this meant getting up early enough to have some quality time with her before I had to get ready for work. In the evenings, I would leave the office by 5:30 p.m., so I could be home by 6:00 p.m. and have a couple of hours with Grace before her bedtime.

However, I would plan to do some work after Grace went to bed. I refer to this as the "transference of hours," which I will discuss as a topic a bit later.

To protect this time with Grace, on my calendar at work, these hours were blocked each day, and it stated "Grace Time" on my calendar. This way, anyone who wanted to schedule time with me saw that this was blocked, and my assistant knew that this was not a time that I would take meetings or calls.

On a rare occasion (maybe a couple of times a year), my assistant would let me know there was someone who really needed to connect with me during this window, and we would figure out whether this was truly the case. Generally, I have found that if you are transparent with the fact that this is time that is blocked to be with your children, then a vast majority of people will respect that this is the case and will agree to another time. In these instances, I would offer to connect after 9:00 p.m. on the same day (or the next day) to ensure I was acknowledging the time sensitivity of the request to connect.

When it comes to weekends, you also need to think about if you are going to allow your work to be a part of your weekend. In general, I have always made it clear that I would not be checking emails or responding to anything until Sunday evening (which is when I choose to prepare for the week ahead). I really tried to protect my Saturdays and a majority of my Sundays for Grace. Over the years, there were weekends when I had to work, but these were very specific times when it was needed, and I tried not to make this a regular occurrence.

Also, it is important to note that, even though I worked on Sunday evenings, I always ensured that my team knew that this is when I chose to prepare for the week and that I did not expect the team to respond and take action during the weekend (unless there was a very specific instance when this was needed). I wanted to ensure that the teams I worked with did not feel they needed to adapt to my way of working to be successful.

I am now working on a team where we are trying to create a culture where we "schedule send" any emails we may be sending on Sunday evening for delivery on Monday morning. This is a great development and one I wholeheartedly support, as it shows respect for protecting everyone's time on the weekend.

THE POWER OF SAYING "NO"

There was guidance I was given late in my career which I wish I had been given much earlier because it is an important point to apply in many aspects of our lives. It is the power to say "No" and not feel like you have to give a reason as to why you are saying "No."

I was speaking with a colleague and telling him that I would not be able to join him for a specific meeting and was sharing the background on the other meeting and why it was important for me to attend. My colleague stopped me and said, "Sarah, you don't need to give me the reason why you can't make it. You just need to say that you can't make it. If you give me a reason, then I am going to make a judgment as to whether you should be attending the meeting I want you to attend versus the other meeting... and that is not my judgment to make. It is your call."

This is some of the most empowering guidance I have been given in terms of managing these moments. In many instances, it is better if we just say that we can't make it and not provide the reason why.

This guidance can apply to work, and it also can apply to your personal life. When you are asked to go to a social commitment and you have a conflict, it is generally easier to just say that you are booked. Do not share what you already have on your calendar, as it may (or may not) be viewed the same by your family or friend who is inviting you to join them.

PRIORITIZING YOUR FAMILY OVER WORK

There are times when your personal and family life will need to be prioritized over your work. Unfortunately, this could come due to unfortunate circumstances (in the form of an illness for you, your child, or a family member, a death in the family/friend group, or divorce). If any of these situations occur, it will undoubtedly shift your focus and affect how you show up at work.

Speaking from personal experience across many of these situations, the most important thing to do is to prioritize what you and your family/friends need in these challenging moments in life. There is nothing more important than being where you need to be and giving the support you need to give to those you love or to yourself.

This can be easier said than done, but what I have found over the course of my career is that those you work with will be there to support you during these challenging times in life. The important part is to articulate what you can or can't handle from a work standpoint as you are going through this difficult time.

THE FINE LINES OF PHYSICAL BOUNDARIES

There are a range of things to think through when it comes to creating physical boundaries relating to parenting and your work.

This can be even more challenging when working from home is either a significant part of your work reality or induced by a pandemic (whoever thought that would be a common thing to say?) or by your children being home sick and you needing to be home with them for a period of time.

Regardless of the reason for working from home, figure out what works for you in terms of creating the needed physical boundaries so that your work does not distract you from what you need to do as a parent, and vice versa.

To be clear, this is probably one of the biggest challenges we face these days as the two worlds have been merged more than ever... which is why it is essential to figure out the operating model that works for you and your family.

It is clear that our ability to protect our homes from being infiltrated by our working world is so different compared to growing up watching our parent(s) go off to work each day.

The shift to a hybrid working model has also made it tougher to figure out where to draw the lines in protecting our children from being exposed to our work (whether we want them to be or not).

There are a range of things you need to think through in terms of how you want to integrate work into your home life, as it will define many aspects of how you are managing the juggling act on a day-to-day basis. It is important to figure out how to set physical boundaries between work and home so you can have quality time with your family and also focus on your work when you need to when working from home.

WHERE, WHEN, & HOW YOU GET YOUR WORK DONE

The question of where you get your work done has become a topic of significant discussion in recent years, and the ability to get our work done in a virtual world has also been discussed at length.

The evaluation of where we will do work is going to continue for the foreseeable future, as the "future of work" discussions continue to reflect on where society is heading with our collective view on work and how it fits into our lives.

The decision about working from home versus working from the office is both a personal decision and a company decision, meaning that a company can set a policy for where we work and how often we need to be there. Then, as individuals, we need to also reflect on where we do our best work.

My only counsel is to really think through what your optimal scenario is for managing your family and your work, and do what you can to design your life to match that scenario. Just realize that the scenario that you design for the early stages of your children's lives may need to shift over time, so it is important to be flexible and adjust as needed to define when, where, and how you get your work done, while still being there for your family.

TO HAVE A HOME OFFICE (OR NOT)

This may seem like an easy topic to think through, but it is important to determine if you want to have a proper home office set up in your home or whether you would prefer not to.

I actually never had a goal of working from home, so I did not strive to set up a home office.

This meant when I did work from home at night (or during the pandemic), our kitchen table was essentially my home office.

There are pros and cons to having a home office, and this is a very personal decision. The only thing I would recommend doing is thinking through what you want to achieve by having a home office and whether it helps (or hurts) the boundaries you are trying to set for yourself when it comes to raising your children and working.

Due to the pandemic, the reality of the hybrid model has fundamentally changed how we view working from home, and, for many, having a home office is now essential.

If the need for a home office is a "must-have" in your world, then it is key to figure out the optimal home office set-up when working from home.

Even though I had never had a desire to work from home or have a home office, during a recent move, I decided that I needed to create a home office, due to the hybrid nature of my workweek.

This was new for me, but I have found that I now enjoy having the option of working from home in an office that is set up just how I want to work.

FIND A CUPBOARD

This guidance will make sense only if you work outside of your home and commute to and from work.

If you do work outside of the home and you carry your laptop to and from work, then one of the recommendations that I would make is to find a cupboard or a closet where you can place your laptop bag (including the laptop) when you get home from work.

The practice of putting your laptop away when you get home helps on a range of fronts. If it sits out on the counter, or your laptop bag sits in view, then it can be a distraction for you, when you are meant to be home focused on your children.

This may seem like a small thing, but think about how little time you actually get to spend with your children during the average weekday. Any time that you are distracted is quality time that is taken away from the interactions with your children.

We also have a cupboard where we charge our phones. Although I must admit that it has been harder over the years to put the phone in the cupboard as it has become our "remote control" for operating various technologies within our home.

However, I still did not check my email on my phone until after Grace went to bed, which took some self-control. This was always well worth it, as we had quality time together each evening.

I completely appreciate that the dynamics have changed for many working parents who are now working in a hybrid model. If you work from home (for any period of time), give some thought to how you create a finite "end" to your day in order to be present with your children. This could mean that you make a point to shut your home-office door or you remove your laptop from the kitchen counter and put it away.

It is important to figure out how to set physical boundaries between work and home to the best of your ability, given the two worlds you are trying to manage each day.

BUILD A COMPARTMENTALIZATION MUSCLE

The approach you take to setting mental boundaries may be one of the most important sets of boundaries you define as you are starting out as a working parent. The challenge of setting mental boundaries is that it requires you to build a muscle that many of us do not naturally have built into our DNA.

We have all been told that we need strong "core" muscles, but no one talks about a key mental muscle... the compartmentalization muscle.

This muscle enables you to focus on what you need to focus on at any given time, whether it is being present with your children for the few hours you have together in the evening or being present during a meeting with your team.

There can be times when your personal life and work life intersect and/or overlap. This is completely fine and is definitely going to happen, but there are times when you are purposely trying to keep things separate in order to focus. This is where your compartmentalization muscle needs to flex.

The most important time to try to flex your compartmentalization muscle is when you are trying to spend quality time with your children and there is something at work that is pulling at your attention. Try to do what you can to be present with your children, and address the work demand once you have a window to do so. For example, when your children are napping or asleep for the night or watching a video for a little while, you can then address the work-related demand.

Some people naturally have a strong compartmentalization muscle, and others need to work on building this muscle. It is actually a muscle you can build and strengthen with practice. There is a learning curve with developing this muscle, but, with work, it can be done.

TRANSFERENCE OF HOURS

The concept of "transference of hours" will depend on the type of job you are in, the amount of work you are required to do in a given day, and whether it is feasible to do some of your work during off-business hours.

My role has generally required me to work longer than the typical workday, so I looked for ways to ensure I could be there for Grace during the hours that she was awake... and then get some of my work done after she went to sleep.

The challenge with this approach is that you need to ensure that you are also making time for yourself, your spouse/partner, and your friends. On a regular basis, check in on how you are doing in terms of managing the transference of hours. See if you need any adjustments to the approach you are taking to accomplish everything you want in your day-to-day life.

FINDING TIME FOR YOU

One of the biggest challenges as a working parent is finding time for yourself. It is easier said than done, but it is essential to figure out how to carve out time for whatever you need to do to recharge. This can be taking a walk, working out, getting a massage, or going for a mani/pedi... something that is for you, and something that makes you feel good.

This is generally the thing that working parents do not prioritize, but we need to do what we can for ourselves each day or week (at a minimum). If we do not find the time for and put ourselves into our schedule, no one will do it for us.

THE GIFT OF TREATING YOURSELF

Finding time for yourself should be part of your daily or weekly routine... and the gift of treating yourself is when you carve out a significant amount of time to do what you want to do, whether it is a weekend away with friends or a day at the spa. These "gifts" are moments in the year when you give yourself the gift of time to do what you want, without the requirements of juggling your children, career, or household demands.

Think of these moments as gifts that are non-returnable or non-cancellable. Once you confirm what you want to do, ensure that you give yourself the gift you deserve.

THE LUXURY OF HAVING TIME TO READ

Besides sleep, the other thing that many parents say is hard to fit into the day-to-day is time to read. Many parents say it feels like a luxury to sit down and read a book, which I can relate to, given my own experience.

Personally, I found that it was very hard to find the time to read during my juggling act years unless I was on vacation.

Due to my busy schedule, I tended to read magazine articles or books that were broken up into topics and did not require me to remember what I had read the last time I had picked up that book. Otherwise, I spent time having to re-read the prior chapter to remind myself where I was in the book, which was frustrating.

Another good option for "reading" is to listen to an audiobook during your commute or workout. It is not quite the same as curling up with a good book on your sofa, but it does allow you to keep up with those things you want to read.

Hopefully, you can find the time to read what you want to read, but I just want to recognize that this is one of those things that can be a challenge, given all that you are juggling each day.

LEAD BY EXAMPLE

When you think about the concept of leading by example, there are two different groups who are watching you each day...

Your children have a front-row seat to your juggling act. They can see how it is going and whether you are enjoying the various aspects of your life, so take note of the example you are setting.

There is also another group watching you... other young people who are thinking about how they will juggle a career and a family when they decide to have children someday. They are observing the various examples of parents they work with and how they are managing the juggling act.

Leading by example can take many different forms, and, on certain days, we may lead by example better than on others. Always be aware that, when you are a working parent, you are showing the next generation of working parents and your children (especially your daughters) what it looks like to be a working parent. This will inform their decisions about whether they want to try to follow that path in the future.

TAKE A MOMENT
TO REFLECT...

BUILDING YOUR
SUPPORT NETWORK

One of the most important things as you embark on being a working parent is to have a support network in place that can help you along the way.

There are different roles that different parts of your support network will play over time. The goal is to have a range of support to lean on as needed.

As one of my friends shared, "Overinvest in help. It truly takes a village and ensures you have the right support structure in place. It is an investment in yourself, your family, and your career."

FAMILY DYNAMICS

If you have family who live nearby and can be a support to you, that is always helpful. However, it is important to understand what level of support they truly want to provide in your day-to-day life. This will obviously vary by family, but it is always worth exploring what is feasible in terms of support from family members.

I have seen situations where extended family have been incredibly helpful in supporting family members who need some extra help with carpool pickup or watching children after school.

However, I have also heard stories of extended family members living close to each other but not providing any extra help. There can be good reasons that this is the case, and it is definitely not a given.

So, the key point is to clearly understand what your extended family members are willing to do when it comes to providing support to you and your family.

PHONE A FRIEND

At the beginning of your children's lives, it is helpful to build a network of friends who work flexible schedules and stay-at-home parents (who are supportive of what you are trying to juggle, as defined earlier under "Different Types of Parents").

When you have identified your friends who have flexible schedules or are staying at home (and are willing to be there to help when needed), they are truly lifesavers. This can range from ensuring you understand any dynamics that may be happening at school that you were not aware of because you are not able to spend much time there due to your work demands... to being willing to pick up your children from school at the last minute (when your nanny is sick).

I truly valued my stay-at-home mom friends who were there for me along the journey of raising Grace. If I ever needed anything, they were always just a phone call or text away, which was so appreciated.

In terms of support from other working parents, this will generally come in the form of moral support versus actually being able to help you in any way, since your friends who are also working parents are in the midst of their own juggling act on a daily basis.

However, working parents are a great resource when you are looking for leads on nannies or other resources that could help you with your day-to-day juggling act.

NEIGHBORS YOU CAN COUNT ON

The need for supportive neighbors is truly a must when you are a working parent and especially if you are a single working parent.

Hopefully, you have neighbors who can be there to unlock your house when your nanny and children are inadvertently locked out of the house (and ideally they have your spare key)... or they help you carry out your Christmas tree to the curb... or bring in your packages when you are traveling... the list of helpful moments where your neighbors can help you is long.

Depending on where you live and how friendly and welcoming your neighborhood is, one thing to think about is the effort you make in getting to know your neighbors.

We were fortunate to live in what my mom would refer to as a "cup of sugar" neighborhood. If you were baking something and needed an egg or a cup of sugar, you could call a neighbor and run next door and get whatever you needed.

We had amazing neighbors who became like family to us over the years, and the love and support they showed to both Grace and me is one of our fondest memories of living in that special neighborhood.

CONFIRM THE CHILDCARE YOU NEED

One of the essential considerations when becoming a working parent is to have the right childcare support in place... do not underestimate your need for support.

The first thing to determine is what level of childcare support you need.

From our standpoint, we have always had a nanny (since Grace was twelve weeks old).

There are many options when it comes to childcare support... daycare, after-school programs, relatives, friends, nanny-share scenarios, and au pairs. Just recognize that you will need help, so you will just need to figure out the best scenario that works for you.

In this section, I am going to go deeply into the details about hiring and managing a nanny, as this was my experience, and I have been asked for detailed advice on this topic over the years. There is other guidance out in the world that you can research if you are looking for details about the other types of childcare options noted above.

In addition, there may also be a need for additional "support" with the house. If you are hiring a nanny, consider hiring a nanny who is also capable of being a "house manager." They should be able to handle laundry, meal preparation, grocery shopping, dry cleaners, managing home-repair appointments, etc... whatever it is that you need to make your life work on a daily basis. This is essential when you are trying to juggle raising your children, running a household, and managing a career as well.

HIRING A NANNY

There are various sources for finding nanny candidates, including word of mouth from friends and colleagues, online resources, and nanny-hiring agencies.

Over the years, I have used all of these sources to find nannies.

One key thing to remember in this process is not to put pressure on yourself to find a nanny that will be with you until your children are in college.

I have seen a range of scenarios unfold over the years with our nannies as well as with my friends who have hired nannies or au pairs.

I do have a friend who hired a nanny, and she was with them from the time her son was born until he went off to college. However, I have had many friends who have had multiple nannies over the course of their children's lives.

We actually had eight different nannies over the course of Grace's growing up years (from age 12 weeks to 18). It ended up that, at around the two-year mark, each nanny had a life change that required them to leave us and move on with their lives (e.g., having a baby of their own, joining the Peace Corps, moving cities to go to graduate school, having a husband who was in the FBI and was transferred to another city). At these transition points, we always took the time to pause and assess what we really needed from our nanny, so that, when we went into the next nanny search, we were able to find a nanny who was appropriate for our collective needs (both Grace's needs and what we were needing from a household-support standpoint).

There can actually be nannies who are a good fit for different stages of your children's life, so don't feel the pressure to feel like you need to hire "the one."

There will be a point when you need to decide if you need a nanny full-time or part-time. This will then determine the type of nanny candidates that you would consider.

A full-time nanny is going to have different expectations from you regarding compensation. If you are their sole source of income, then determine how you want to structure the compensation you are agreeing to. Are you planning to pay them a salary or pay by the hour? Are you paying them for vacation days? Are you paying them for holidays? There is a list of questions you need to be prepared to answer when you are hiring a full-time nanny, so ensure that you think through these questions prior to engaging in a compensation discussion with your nanny candidates.

In the early days, you need a nanny who is going to be completely focused on your child... and I always said in the early days of Grace's life that anything relating to Grace was the priority. However, this can shift over time, as your children go to school, and you decide how you want to use your nanny's time.

Our very first nanny made it clear to us that she was all about raising newborns to one-year-olds, and then she liked to move on. When we hired her, she had already been with seven different families and helped to raise seven different newborns. She ended up staying with us until Grace was two, and then she went and had five children of her own.

It is also important to consider the type of individual that you want to hire. When we were looking for nannies, we looked for individuals who would bring a different perspective or experience to Grace's life. This led us to hire nannies with a range of life experience. One nanny was getting her Master's in Psychology, one was taking classes to prepare to apply to medical school, and one ran her own business (which she was able to do while Grace was in school). In each of these instances, the nanny could still be there to pick Grace up and be with her in the evenings until we got home.

There is a point when you can potentially shift to a part-time nanny. The various nannies I mentioned above were all part-time for us, as they were also managing other things in their lives from either a school or career standpoint. However, a part-time nanny is able to handle picking up your children from school, taking them to any after-school activities/sports, and then getting them home to focus on homework until you get home in the evening. Our part-time nannies also ran errands as needed throughout the week, which was incredibly helpful.

This highlights a key point to reflect on... you and your children will have different needs at different stages of your lives, so finding a nanny who fits well with those needs is essential.

INTERVIEWING NANNY CANDIDATES

In terms of actually interviewing and making a final decision on the nanny, my husband and I always interviewed for a new nanny together (even after we were divorced when Grace was seven years old). This ensured that we were both comfortable with the individual who would be spending time with Grace.

We have also always included Grace in the nanny-interviewing process, as we think it is important that she has a say in who she will be spending time with each day.

When we were interviewing nanny candidates, I had a two-step approach. The first step was a screening interview by phone. I have a list of questions that I would ask the candidate (see example list in Appendix).

If the nanny candidate passed the phone screen, then I would have them come to meet us at the house.

During this interview at the house, we shared with the nanny candidate a nanny overview (see example in Appendix). This outlined our expectations for this role across a range of topics, including our parenting philosophy, specific duties of the role, approach to discipline, and day-to-day things like meals/snacks guidance.

This nanny overview was a very helpful point of reference during the interview, because it basically covered all of the topics that we would want to discuss with a potential nanny and helped to guide our discussion.

There is, potentially, not a more-important hiring decision you can make in your life in terms of who will be helping you to raise your child. Being prepared for this discussion and ensuring you cover all of the points you want to understand during the interview is fundamental to finding the right nanny for your family.

MANAGING A NANNY

Between you and your partner, be clear on who will manage your nanny in terms of confirming hours, paying each week, and communicating children's activity schedules.

On Sunday evenings, I would put together a list of reminders for the week and would have that to review with the nanny on Monday morning to kick off the week.

How you want to transition in and out of your day with your nanny also requires some consideration. Given the limited time I had with Grace, I did not want to spend a ton of time chatting with my nanny at the end of the day, so I would ask for a quick debrief on the day, and then she would leave so that Grace and I could have our time together. Again, this is a personal preference in terms of how much time you want to spend with the nanny debriefing on the details of the day. However, I just viewed it as time being taken away from my quality time with Grace, so I tried to keep our transitions brief.

The other tool that helped to make our transitions as focused as possible was that, in the early days of Grace's life, we had a nanny log, where the nanny could provide any notes on the day in terms of how Grace was doing. When she was an infant, this would note how many bottles she had and how long she had slept for her naps. As she got older, the log would note any new words or funny quotes from the day or anything else the nanny would want us to be aware of from Grace's day.

STAYING IN TOUCH WITH PAST NANNIES

If you have had nannies who have moved on, but who left on positive terms and still wanted to be in your children's lives, they can be an incredible support to call upon when needed.

Grace is actually close to a number of her past nannies, who have continued to stay in touch with her over the years. They are considered close family friends, and we feel fortunate to have them in our lives.

FINDING RELIABLE BABYSITTERS

Even if you have a nanny you use during the week, it can be helpful also to have a few babysitters you are able to call when you need coverage on a weekend day or evening. There are a range of sources for good babysitters (word of mouth from friends, your children's preschool teachers, or various sitter sites where you can screen sitters and then meet with them).

Depending on the age of your children, there are various types of sitters who can stay with your children. The important point is to find individuals who you are comfortable leaving your children with and whom your children enjoy spending time with for a couple of hours. In certain instances, these two things do not match up, and, even though you are comfortable with the babysitter, your children do not enjoy spending time with them. Stay open to this feedback from your children, as it makes it much easier for all of you if they are excited for who is coming to stay with them when you are heading out for an evening.

There are also sitters who are better suited for different stages of your children's lives. When your children get a bit older, generally, they want someone who is fun to be with, who they can relate to, and who will do age-appropriate things with them. It is also helpful to have a babysitter who can drive if there are times that they are watching your children and they need to be picked up or taken somewhere.

Also, at a minimum, I would recommend having a babysitter (or your nanny) booked each week for a standing date night for you and your spouse/partner (or, if you are single, so that you can go out on dates or out with a friend).

A reliable babysitter is definitely an important part of your support network, so invest the time to find ones you can trust.

OUTSOURCING AS MUCH AS POSSIBLE

There are some key themes that you will hear me come back to throughout this book, and one of them is the concept of "outsource what you need to in order to make your life run." This obviously has a socio-economic consideration that comes with it. However, there is a cost/value equation when it comes to your time as a working parent, so you will need to determine where it makes sense to engage incremental support (whom you pay) versus incremental support that you lean on (such as a family member or friend).

There are so many logistics of life that need to be managed when you are running a household as a working parent. The juggling act requires you to get organized on the logistics of life, from carpool schedules, to scheduling doctor appointments, to who is going to drop off the returns to UPS.

In addition to childcare or a nanny, there are a number of key needs when running a household. The suggestions below regarding engaging additional resources to help you will require funding that may not be feasible due to your financial situation. However, I just wanted to highlight these roles that can make things easier for you if you can afford to put them in place to help manage the logistics of your life.

CLEANING SERVICE

The frequency of a cleaning service can vary from weekly, to bi-weekly, to monthly. If you can afford to have someone come in and help you handle some of the cleaning duties, it can make a substantial difference in terms of keeping your house clean.

HANDYMAN

Depending on how handy you and/or your spouse/partner are when it comes to fixing things around the house, it can be helpful to have someone you can call when you need help around the house. I have a very reliable handyman whom I can call at any time to help with a range of household needs.

YARD SERVICE

The frequency of a yard service can also vary. However, if you can afford to have a service who can manage maintaining your yard... this is one less thing you have to do on the weekends, when you are trying to squeeze in errands between your children's various activities.

HOUSE MANAGER

This can be handled either by your nanny or by someone who focuses only on what is needed in terms of running the house, such as laundry, meal preparation, grocery shopping, dry cleaning (drop-off/pick-up), or dropping off returns to UPS/FedEx/USPS. The list of errands can vary by the week, but there are always errands to be run. There are also home-repair appointments such as meeting the plumber for an unexpected plumbing issue, which a house manager can handle for you.

In general, all of these resources are paid either a fixed rate for service or an hourly rate. For example, I have hired house managers that I just pay by the hour to run errands and is some of the best money I could spend, because I am not a fan of making those runs to UPS to handle my online shopping returns.

LOGISTICS OF LIFE

There are so many logistics of life to manage when you are a working parent, and the only way that I have found to keep up with the logistics is to be extremely organized.

I had a number of approaches for managing the various details in life, from all of the key documents, to our home calendar, to the various lists I made to keep track of all of the details. I will share these approaches in the coming sections.

My friend suggested automating as much as you can. She reflected on the fact that we need to constantly be asking ourselves the question... "Is this worth my time, or is there some other way to get this task done?" Given how precious our time is with our children, we need to focus less time on the low-value stuff in life and more on the things that matter.

Over the years, I joked that I am a "relaxed Type A," which some people who know me would say is debatable. However, I will still claim this is the best explanation of how I approached managing my life as a working parent. I am wired to be organized, but I have also had to relax on certain things over the years that may not be as organized as I would like... as this is a reality of the juggling act.

My favorite example of this is what I mention in another section around keeping up with photos I had taken of Grace over the years. I found this to be one of the challenges I was never fully on top of. However, at some point, I just told myself not to worry about it... that there were plenty of photos of Grace even if I did not feel they were organized in the way I wanted them to be.

ORGANIZE DETAILS TO KEEP YOUR LIFE RUNNING

There are a wide range of details that you need to keep for easy reference relating to your life. This can range from Social Security numbers, to passports, to frequent-flier program details.

As you organize these details, ensure you keep all of the key documents in a central place (or consider capturing all relevant details in one document) that you can access easily, as you will end up needing to refer to them over the years, and it is helpful to have them all in one place.

CREATE A HOME CALENDAR

When trying to manage your children's lives, it is helpful to keep one calendar that both parents (and nanny, if one is involved in your children's lives) can view and manage as needed. This way, each parent can work off the same understanding of where the children are each day as well as keep everything straight in terms of school and extracurricular activities.

A Google calendar has worked well for us. We all have access to it (including our nanny), but there are many calendar options these days that can help a family manage these details.

We generally end up having a discussion about once a month to run through calendar-related items. This ensures that we are aligned on any changes or shifts that are taking place in the calendar.

Some families have a major need for this type of calendar to manage all of the details, especially when multiple children are involved with a wide range of activities taking place on a day-to-day basis. While this may not be needed for certain families, if you are co-parenting and/or there is a nanny involved in helping to manage your children's schedules, this approach to managing the calendar works very well to ensure that everyone is clear on what is happening in your children's lives and when.

TO DO LISTS

Admittedly, my To Do lists are essential to my day. I have a personal To Do list that I keep on my phone in a To Do list app, and it helps to ensure that all of the important details in my personal life are in view.

My work To Do list is separate from my personal To Do list, and this is purposeful, as I do not want to be looking at the other To Do list at times when I am trying to focus on things in my personal life or in my professional life.

There was a day when my To Do list had disappeared from my phone, and I was getting tech support to try to retrieve it. I told the tech guy that I could not even remember all that was listed on my To Do list and he said, "This is because when you write it down on your To Do list, it gives you the permission to forget." When he shared this with me, I found it to be completely true. When I write things down on my To Do list, they are then out of my brain and on that list.

THE SUNDAY LIST

Throughout any given week, there are a myriad of things that come up that require your attention as a parent. The permission slip that needs to be signed, the medical insurance form that needs to be submitted, or the baby gift that needs to be ordered for your friend who lives in another city.

The advice I generally give to new parents is to put all of those items on a list for Sunday. Then spend a concentrated one to two hours getting through the list, versus trying to squeeze in tackling these items on the list throughout the week. Unless something is time sensitive (and there is always something that is), it worked better for me to just try to tackle these items in one focused session instead of feeling like I was trying to squeeze them in during my workday or during my time with Grace.

The key to this game plan is to ensure that your children are taken care of for this period of time that you are trying to tackle your list, whether they are spending time with your spouse/partner, playing with friends, napping, or taking a little time to watch a video. This will enable you to focus and get through your list as quickly as possible.

NANNY REMINDERS LIST

One of the tools I used to manage the week with my nanny was to keep a "reminders list," which was essentially a To Do list, but it had all of the various reminders that I wanted to ensure stayed in view in a given week. This can seem basic, but anytime anything came up during the week, I would just note it down on the reminders list. This ensured that we were keeping up with all of the moving pieces that needed to be managed in Grace's life (and in our life) each week.

PLAN YOUR MEALS FOR THE WEEK

If you can take the time, it does help to look ahead at the week and figure out your meal game plan for the week. This can be a combo of cooking, ordering in, and eating out. When cooking, always have some simple recipes that you can throw together for a quick meal. There are also the home food delivery services that are worthwhile checking out.

The goal is to make weeknight meals as easy as possible. This starts with outlining your grocery list for the week.

My friend shared that she kept a running grocery list... and whenever she ran out of something or noticed the supply was getting low, she would add it to her grocery list right then to make sure she did not forget to pick it up the next time she was at the store. There is also the option of using an online grocery delivery service to capture your running grocery list.

There is also the option to auto-subscribe for those things you need on a regular basis and have things delivered right to your home.

For those of us who shop at the same grocery store each week, there is something to outlining your grocery list in the order of the store. As you walk through it, you can efficiently shop for the various items that you need on a weekly basis. This will not work for those one-off items that you need only once a year (for holidays or when you need to make your child's birthday cake). However, it does make your grocery visit as efficient as possible.

HANDLING THE MAIL

One of the things that can visually pile up and make you feel that you are not in control of things is the mail that arrives each day at your home.

There are a couple of approaches you can take to handling the mail.

My recommendation is to find two minutes to sort through and open the mail each day. Throw away anything you do not need (catalogs, fliers, etc.). Open bills, and put them in a file to pay when you pay your bills (if you are receiving paper bills). Create a space (or file) to put the items for the various things you might need to handle at some point later such as... invitations for birthdays, weddings, or fundraisers. Define a place where you put those catalogs you might want to flip through when you have a spare minute.

In general, clear out as much of the pile of mail as possible on a daily basis, and get rid of the clutter that it can create in your home. This may seem like a minor point, but it is amazing how these small things in our day-to-day lives can make us feel that we are not keeping up with things.

However, you could also find a spot to place the mail each day, which is, ideally, out of sight. Then, you set aside a dedicated time during the week (maybe as part of your Sunday routine) to go through it all.

There are those things that you receive in the mail that you need to attend to in a timely manner... and the rest will probably make it into your recycling bin.

Whatever approach you take, just figure out a routine that works for you.

ONLINE SHOPPING & RETURNS

If you are an online shopper (I actually do 90%+ of my shopping online these days), then you need to figure out the best game plan to manage the array of boxes that come into your home in a given week.

If you have the space to identify a "shipping cupboard or closet," it is helpful as a place to store the boxes until you are ready to deal with them.

It can also be helpful to figure out who can help you handle the inevitable shipping returns, which take time to manage at UPS, FedEx, or USPS. This can range from a responsibility for you (which I think is not ideal), your spouse/partner, one of your children (if they are of driving age), a nanny, a house manager, or a teenager you know who wants to make some extra money (whom you can pay hourly). From my standpoint, I think it is some of the best money you can spend to get help with this task and avoid spending your time standing in line at the UPS store.

PAYING BILLS

One of the things that I tried to build into my schedule was to pay my bills every Sunday. It is never fun to pay bills, but if you set aside a small window every Sunday, then it never becomes a major task, and you can keep up with your finances more easily.

As a working parent, anything that you can do to make yourself more efficient should be a priority. This is where online banking comes in.

Also, depending on how you have divided up your responsibilities within your household with your spouse, this may be a moot point.

Even if your spouse is handling the family finances, I would strongly recommend that you know how to access and use your online banking account.

Now, some of you may receive only online bills, but if you are still receiving paper bills at home, then you may want to create files that help you keep up with the "pending" and "paid" bills each month.

If you are comfortable using autopay to pay your bills online, then this just enables you to set things up to ensure that you don't miss a payment and to avoid having to pay bills each month. I personally do not use autopay because I want to see (and process) what my life is costing each month.

One other suggestion that was a teaching moment was during Grace's senior year in high school, when I had her sit down with me on a few Sundays to help me pay our bills. This helped her to see what our life cost on a monthly basis and how online banking worked. It was important to have her understand "the cost of life" before heading off to college and eventually going out on her own and managing her own expenses.

THE NEVER ENDING LAUNDRY

Doing laundry is always a chore... there is no getting around it. It is safe to say that the laundry basket is never empty for long. The minute you have finished doing the laundry there is something that has been worn that goes into the laundry basket. So, thinking through the schedule you want to put in place that works best for your household is key.

I liked to do laundry on Sunday, as I did not want to be doing laundry every day, while some of my friends would do a load a day, so it never built up. Either way works; just think through what will work best for your family dynamic.

Just remember that there is a point in the future when your children will be able to do their own laundry (Grace started in 6th grade), and that is a huge positive when it happens.

KEEPING UP WITH DOCTORS APPOINTMENTS & FILES

As you are putting together your family calendar, try to note when you need to schedule the various doctor and dentist appointments for your children (and yourself).

As a working parent, it is always a struggle to figure out when you can block out hours on your calendar at work to fit in these appointments, but it is essential for your children and yourself.

One routine I tried was to schedule Grace's annual appointment for the days right after her birthday, which was helpful because it was always a time in the year when I prioritized being in town.

I also tried to schedule my annual appointments during the summer, when there were fewer demands on my time relating to Grace's school and activities schedule.

Once you have set up those doctor/dentist appointments, then do everything you can to protect them (and not move them just because an "important" meeting comes up).

I have spoken to many working parents who prioritize their children's various appointments but have canceled their own appointments. This is not a good trend, because we need to take care of ourselves... full stop.

KEEPING UP WITH HEALTH INSURANCE FILING

This is another not-so-favorite task (right up there with paying bills). However, ensure that you put this on your list to handle in a timely manner if you are required to submit insurance forms in order to receive reimbursement from your health-insurance company.

At the point when Grace was old enough (freshman year in high school), I had her fill out the forms that were related to her doctor/dentist appointments, so she could start to understand what it truly means to receive medical insurance coverage.

THE JOYS OF SUMMER SCHEDULING

As working parents, when summer approaches there is the need to figure out how your children are going to spend the summer. If you have a full time nanny, then you will have the coverage you need throughout the summer. However, if you are dependent on daycare or school plus after-school programs for coverage, then it can be daunting to think about how to ensure your children are taken care of all summer long.

There are many ways to structure this summer coverage. It will most likely take a combination of summer activities and/ or summer camps, vacation time as a family and potentially family visits (from grandparents who want to spend some quality time with their grandchildren).

The best guidance I can share is to try to plan ahead and think through the combination of summer activities that will work for you and your children. Each summer may be different in terms of how your children want to spend their summer. There are a range of summer activities your children can participate in from swim team to attending an art or theater class to day camps. The list of potential activities is long and will change given the age of your children. As your children get a little older, they may want to go to sleep-away camp (for a week, month or longer).

There is also the consideration of how your children will get to/from all of these summer activities. Depending on your situation, the need for carpools or finding a driver to shuttle your children to/from summer activities is also a consideration (depending on the flexibility of your job and the ability to drive your children to their various summer activities).

Summertime is meant to be fun for you and your children... and hopefully you can enjoy special moments together throughout the summer. However, I must admit that most of the working parents I have known over the years, would get to a point in the summer and could not wait to have their children go back to school in the Fall. This was because the wiring together of summer activities was always a challenging time of the year when managing the juggling act.

TRAVELING TESTS

One of the decisions that we made when we had Grace is that we would travel early and often with her, so that she would be accustomed to traveling (and this included car and plane travel). We made her first cross-country flight from Atlanta to Los Angeles at eight weeks old to visit my parents (and she has been traveling ever since).

I joked that it takes four-plus hours to run a marathon, and this first flight was four-plus hours. By the end of the flight, I was exhausted and felt like I had run a marathon even though I had been sitting in an airline seat the entire time.

It goes without saying that it is not easy to travel with an infant or young child and it can be a true test in patience as a parent.

The "tests" start with all of the items that you need to pack and bring on a trip when you have little ones (which seems to have increased exponentially over the years). Then, there is the potential change in time zones (depending on where you are traveling to), which can impact your children's sleep patterns. Next, there are the new sleeping arrangements (not sleeping in their own crib/bed) that your children need to adjust to wherever you are staying on your trip. Also, there is the challenge of being out of their daily routines (in terms of eating, naptime, or bedtime). Finally, there is the potential of being completely spoiled by family members you may be visiting on your trip. All of these elements play into a trip being more stressful than it should be (especially if it is meant to be a vacation).

It is important to adjust your expectations when traveling with your young children. These trips (which may be referred to as a vacation) are not for you. They are for your children and for the family members that you are visiting so they can see your children. The lack of rules and structure that accompanies these trips will not ruin your children for life. Learn to let go during these times, and just try to enjoy the time together as a family. There will be rewiring needed after you return from these types of trips, but that is just one of those things.

Even with all of these factors in play, it is still worth it to take the trips as early and often as you can to build your "traveling stamina" because the sooner you figure it out... the sooner it becomes easier for all involved.

MANAGING PHOTOS

The one area that I did not do well in when it came to organization during Grace's childhood was managing the gazillion
photos we took of her. If I were to say one thing as you are
becoming a parent… figure out what your strategy is for
managing photos.

These days, we have all of our photos on our phones, so it is
much easier than when I was raising Grace and you actually
had your photos printed (I am clearly dating myself with this
reflection). Try to select your favorites each week, and put
them in a folder so you can find them when you want to
show them to others. Also, make sure you have backed up
your photos, as it is a huge bummer if you lose photos of your
children due to unforeseen technical issues.

This may sound like an easy thing to do, but with everything
you have going on, sometimes these easy things become
bigger tasks if you have not kept up with it along the way.

GIFT GIVING STRATEGY

There are certain phases in life when you feel you are constantly buying gifts... the wedding phase, the baby-shower phase, and the never-ending children's birthday party phase.

Regardless of the phase, it can be helpful to think about what you can do to make buying gifts for these moments as simple and straightforward as possible.

For example, when it comes to children's birthday parties, if you find a gift that is a favorite for a specific age or gender, buy a couple of the items, and have them on hand to wrap up as needed. It can definitely help when it seems like you are going to a birthday party almost every weekend.

The same can go for baby gifts. If you find a gift you love giving, you can always give the same gift to various friends around the country.

There is also a point when you may decide you want to simplify your gift giving (for holidays or friends' birthdays) and discuss with your family and friends what makes sense to do instead of giving gifts to recognize the moment.

THE POWER OF
ROUTINES

There is something powerful (and magical) about setting some specific routines in your life that enable you to fit in all that you want to fit in as a working parent. There are different types of routines that can help you structure your weekdays or your weekends. There is a benefit to thinking about where you can establish a routine that you and your family get used to and ultimately makes day-to-day life easier.

MANAGING WEEKDAYS

The reality is that the weekdays are the true test of the juggling act... this is when you are always going to feel the most stretched between your family commitments and your work commitments, and it never feels like there are enough hours in the day for either world.

There is an invaluable balance to be gained by putting a schedule in place and then being flexible with what happens on any given day. Even with being as organized as possible, almost every day, there will be something (and, on some days, many things) that do not go as planned. It is how we react in those moments that enables us to either enjoy our lives or get frustrated by the juggling act.

At each stage of your children's lives, from infant, to toddler, to pre-school, to grade school, to middle school and high school, the weekday schedule will change. Also, what is needed from you as a parent will change, from being hands-on to being consciously hands-off as your children prepare to leave the nest and head out into the world. It is a matter of recognizing when these shifts need to occur and adjusting accordingly to what your children (and you) need during the weekdays in order to effectively juggle all that happens on any given weekday.

The routines you put in place for your weekdays with your children will help you to manage all that you are trying to squeeze into the hours you spend together, from how you wake them up and get them ready for the day, to how you handle breakfast, to how you all handle getting out the door in the morning. It sets a tone for the day for all of you. So, think about what you want this time to feel like in terms of starting your day.

The same goes for the routines in the evening, when you are all together again, from getting homework done, to making dinner, to bathtime, to getting ready for bed, and any bedtime rituals you have with your children. Give some thought to how you want this time to feel as you are ending your day with your children.

Admittedly, as working parents, you are generally exhausted by the time you get to the end of the day and try to get everything done before putting your children to bed at a reasonable hour.

So, whatever routines you can put in place will help all of you to know what is expected from the morning or evening and allow you to enjoy these moments together as much as possible.

MANAGING WEEKENDS

When you are trying to manage the juggling act, you need to think about how you are using your weekends to connect with your family, get the things done you need for life to work, and find some time for yourself to recharge and have some fun. This is a very tall order for a 48+ hour period, so it takes some strategic planning to come out of a weekend feeling connected, accomplished, and refreshed.

Here are some suggestions for how to structure your weekend. Please take these as one person's view of what worked, as there are many other models you can consider, depending on the demands of your life. Putting some thought into it can help make the weekends be the best they can be.

Heading into the weekend, think about whether you and your partner/spouse want to figure out who is going to get a little extra sleep each morning. Figure out who gets to "sleep in" (which may be only an extra hour, but every hour counts)... and who gets up with your children to make breakfast and get the day started.

We generally each took a morning with Grace while the other was able to get a little extra sleep... which was much needed and helped both of us to re-charge our batteries over the course of the weekend.

Friday nights - I have always viewed Friday nights as family time for a couple of reasons. First of all, I was generally so tired from the week that the thought of going out did not seem appealing. Secondly, it was important to reconnect with

Grace after a busy week. We did have some fun Friday-night traditions that I will share a little later.

Saturdays - In general, Saturdays are an "all hands on deck" type of day. If you have children, it is a combination of attending sporting events, birthday parties, and playdates... while squeezing in some must-do errands between various commitments.

When it comes to running errands, think through whether bringing your children along will be a positive experience for all involved or a stressful one (more to come on this in the next section on "Weekends = Errands").

Saturday nights - Ideally, you will have the energy to do something social (with adults) on Saturday night... so you can either have a date night with your spouse/partner or go out to dinner with friends. Having something planned for Saturday night helped me feel that I had a social life.

Sundays - Generally, a combination of church (if you are the churchgoing type), getting things done around the house (cleaning, laundry, gardening/yardwork), and meal prep for the week ahead. As mentioned earlier, I also tried to carve out one hour each Sunday to deal with all of the house-related bills, responding to invitations, placing online orders, etc.

Sunday nights - The focus on Sunday night is to prepare for the week... getting the children's schedule sorted, writing a list for the nanny/house manager of To Do's, and doing any required work to get ready for the workweek.

Ensure that you are clear on the driving schedule (e.g., school, sports, parties, doctor appointments) and which parent will attend which school/sporting events that week. Get clarity on any extra items needed throughout the week (supplies for projects, costumes for school events, snack duty, birthday gifts, etc.).

When you have young children, and naps are still in your schedule during the weekend, focus on doing things during their naps that you can't get done when they are awake. Try to make the most of this gift of time, which might free you up for doing something for yourself.

For me, sometime on Saturday and Sunday was a good time to work out each day (if possible). One of the must-do's I started prioritizing was getting a weekly massage. This can sound like an extravagance when you are trying to squeeze everything in, but I found it to be essential to help manage my stress and get all of the knots out of my neck and back each week.

As you enter into the weekend, you need to be realistic in terms of what you can accomplish in a given day or weekend. There will always be more things to accomplish on your "To Do" list. Figuring out how to end a weekend feeling connected with your family, accomplished with what you got done to keep life running, and refreshed and ready for the week ahead is a rewarding challenge.

I must admit going into my office on Monday mornings, I breathed a sigh of relief to sit down at my desk and focus on what needed to be done and I could sit in one spot while doing it.

WEEKENDS = ERRANDS

The challenge of being a working parent is that many of the things you need and/or want to get done end up being on your never-ending list on Saturdays and Sundays. This list can be daunting at times when you look at it, so it is important to be realistic about what you can accomplish on any given weekend.

Given all of the demands that come with being a working parent, when you get to the weekend, your "To Do" list on the personal side can take over. You can end up spending your entire weekend trying to get through your list and potentially not spend any quality time with your children.

This was definitely a challenge for me, so my solution was for Grace to join me in running my errands. The positive side of this approach is that we had quality time together in the car talking and singing to the radio, and, in many instances, the errands were related to Grace (e.g., birthday gifts for her friend or a new pair of shoes). However, there were other times when I needed to shop for a new outfit, and Grace would join me at my favorite store and patiently wait as I tried on clothes. However, there were days when I realized that she was being a real trouper for going place to place with me as I checked off the items on my "To Do" list.

This is where a house manager (or your nanny) running certain errands for you during the week will help you to manage the list of errands you need to run in any given weekend. This was an approach I took later in Grace's life. I truly wish I had done so earlier, so we could have spent fewer of our Saturdays driving around running errands.

Also, try to plan your errand route so you can limit your drive time versus crisscrossing town to check things off your list. Review the things you have on your "To Do" list for the weekend, and ask yourself if there is anything that you just don't need to do. Focus on what is most important and figure out if there are ways to get the other things on your list done or let them go completely.

SCHEDULING WEEKEND FUN

This might sound like a given… "Of course, I am going to ensure that my children have fun on the weekends." However, the logistics of life and associated errands can impact how much quality time you actually have to dedicate to fun activities with your children.

It takes conscious effort and some planning, but any time you plan a fun activity or an outing with your children, you are creating fun, positive memories with them. If you can involve your children in the planning of your weekend fun, this enables them to feel a sense of accomplishment when everyone is enjoying the activity together.

BEING SOCIAL

One of the things I made a conscious effort to focus on as a working parent was having friendships from various aspects of my life, from my neighborhood, to Grace's school friends, to my work friends. I always made an effort to schedule evening plans with friends, whether it was going out to a restaurant or having a girlfriend over for dinner and wine (which usually consisted of a special chopped salad I would make and a cheese plate... nothing fancy).

I made a concerted effort to see my friends on a regular basis. This has been a great support for me, as it has helped me stay connected to my girlfriends and has also enabled us to give each other support with whatever is going on in our lives.

One of my girlfriends actually nicknamed my living room "the spa room" because we would relax there after dinner with our wine and solve all of the world's problems, with candles lit and the fire burning.

As a working parent, sometimes our friendships do not get the attention they deserve... especially in the early days of the juggling act. If you can try to carve out the time to see friends along the way, it truly helps you to feel that you have a life outside of raising your children and working.

I completely appreciate that this can be easier said than done, with all that you are trying to fit into a given day or week. However, I can tell you that I never regretted carving out the time for my friendships, as they gave me the fuel I needed as a working mom to continue the juggling act each day.

NURTURING FRIENDSHIPS

As a working parent, one of the things that can go by the wayside quickly is quality time with your friends because you are so busy with the juggling act. It takes effort to foster and maintain meaningful friendships, but it is important to try to make time for your friends as you are also trying to raise your children, work, and do all that you want to do in life.

There is also the dynamic of wanting to maintain friendships you had prior to having children, and this can take a couple of different paths, depending on whether your friends have children or not. For those of your friends who do not have children, you need to think about how you make the effort to see them with and also without your children. Needless to say, it is a very different interaction when you have your children around. Certain friends may want to have quality time with you without your children around.

There are also going to be opportunities to make new friendships throughout your children's life... from school, various activities that they are involved in, or events in your community. This will happen naturally, but, in certain instances, you may need to make a little extra effort. This will entail you taking the initiative to set up time to get together for a playdate with your children or catch up over coffee or drinks/dinner.

My friend reflected on the fact that it is important to find friends who will support you in good times and bad, appreciate you for what you are, don't get upset when you cancel at the last minute, or come in the middle of the night if you are having a crisis.

These are the friendships that you invest in over time, because these friends become a "family of friends" who will love and support you throughout the various stages of your life.

My "family of friends" has been fostered over many years, and I truly value each friendship for its own special connection. With each friendship, I have tried to figure out what will keep us connected and always made the effort to call to catch up or schedule the one-on-one dinner where we could focus on what we needed to share with each other. The phone calls may be right after dropping off for carpool in the morning... and the dinners with a specific friend may take place only every couple of months. It is not about the number of calls or the number of dinners, but the quality of the time you spend together and what you share with each other. Friendships are a gift to yourself, and you should do whatever you can to foster those friendships that are important to you in life.

DATE NIGHT TRADITION

If you are married or in a relationship, scheduling a date night each week (or every other week) is important for your relationship with your spouse/partner, as it gives you time away from your children and allows you to focus on each other.

This can seem like a luxury in the early days of having your children, but it is really essential for the health of your relationship.

Date night can be as casual as heading around the corner to grab a quick bite to eat, getting dressed up for a fun dinner, or heading to the movies.

The other important aspect of date night is that this shows your children that you two go out together and you will come back. There are many parents who do not do this early on in their children's lives... and then their children have separation anxiety from their parents because they have never been left with a babysitter during the evening.

So, figure out what night works for your date night, book the nanny or babysitter, and make your plans to enjoy an evening out without your children.

FRIDAY NIGHT TRADITION

As a working parent, by the time you get to Friday evening, you are exhausted. In the early days of Grace's life, we would have a standing dinner with our close friends at a Mexican restaurant that we walked to from our house. The night was called "Chips & Cheese" (named by Grace and her friend because they basically would eat baskets of chips and cheese even though we ordered them dinner). As parents, we called it the "Decompression Zone," as we would decompress and reflect on our week over margaritas and dinner (and, yes, there were chips, guacamole, salsa, and cheese consumed by the adult table).

Once Grace was older, we transitioned to having movie and sushi nights on Friday nights, which was also fun (and you can see how her taste had evolved from chips and cheese to sushi).

Whatever you decide to do with your Friday nights, just think about whether there is a fun tradition you can create with your children that enables you to spend quality time with them while also decompressing from the week, which is definitely needed.

GIRLS NIGHT TRADITION

There was a special girls night tradition (that I started after my divorce) which was to bring all of my girlfriends together for one evening a year to thank them for their support (initially post-divorce, but then just in terms of the support they provided to me throughout life).

This was always a memorable night... spending time with an amazing group of girls and one of my favorite nights of the year. There is something about putting all of your girlfriends in one place and seeing how they all connect (as some did not know each other well), which was so special.

TAKE A MOMENT
TO REFLECT...

SCHOOL ESSENTIALS

There are a range of things you need to manage when it comes to your children being in school. From figuring out how your children will get to school, to how many school activities you can attend, to attending parent-teacher conferences... the list goes on.

However, with each element, it is helpful to think about how you want to manage these school essentials so you can appropriately engage in your children's lives from preschool through high school. The needs and dynamics around certain elements will change over the years, depending on the age of your children, so you will need to take stock each year in terms of how you are handling each element.

THE SCHOOL DECISION

Depending on where you live and your options for schools for your children, the decision of where to send your children to school can either be straightforward with a well-defined set of schools for your children to attend or there can be a range of school options to consider from public to private.

As you think through the decision of which pre-school to send your children to learn their ABCs , to figuring out which grade school, middle school and high school will be the best fit for your children, the pressure to make the right decision can be a major source of stress.

If you are faced with a range of options to consider, then recommend doing your research, talking to other parents, talking to older children who have gone to the schools you are considering and recognizing that there are schools that are a better fit for some children versus others.

DRIVING CARPOOL

The daily act of driving carpool can seem like a tedious part of our lives, but when I look back on the many years of driving Grace to school each week, we had so many special moments and talks during those drives. Now, the dynamic of carpooling does depend on how many children you have in the car, but that can also make the carpool that much more entertaining.

The important part of these drives to and/or from school is that they can be quality time with your children in a captive environment without the distraction of screens (depending on the age)... and the gift of music, which we always enjoyed during our drives to school. So, ask your children to pick their favorite songs (regardless of their ages). This is a fun time to get exposed to the music they love and to expose them to music you love.

Driving carpool can be the best part of the day, so enjoy this very special time with your children.

ATTENDING CHILDREN'S ACTIVITIES

As a working parent, you will need to decide how often you can attend your children's school activities (whether it is sports, theater, or clubs).

There will always be the expectation that we will be there to support our children when the actual sporting event or school play takes place. Hopefully, you have enough control of your work schedule to make it to some or all of your children's activities.

There was a point where I was trying to leave work a little early to watch Grace play in a golf tournament, but colleagues needed to talk to me urgently. I shared with them that as long as they could handle me talking very quietly on the phone in the golf cart following Grace and her teammates, then I could connect with them. This call was with two younger female colleagues, and they thanked me for the call but also, more importantly, for showing them that prioritizing my child's golf tournament was possible, even while managing the demands of my work schedule. These are the moments when we can show that, although it is a juggling act, it is possible to manage both worlds.

Our working lives can be busy, and it can be hard to make all of the various events. Do whatever you can to make as many as possible. Your children deserve to look out and see you sitting there, smiling at them, and cheering them on in whatever activity they are engaged in.

KEEPING UP WITH SCHOOL DETAILS

When children are in preschool and grade school, there are a lot of things that are sent home in hard copy. When children are older, most of the correspondence from school is via email, so it can be easier to keep up with.

As the various papers and artwork come into the house, figure out a game plan for dealing with all of these papers. If you can, set aside a couple of minutes each night to look at the papers and determine which ones are worth holding on to and which ones need to be quietly thrown away.

I started a system where I went to The Container Store and bought letter-sized boxes for each year of Grace's school. I would selectively place specific stories or artwork in the box for safekeeping and decided which ones needed to go into the trash bag that I kept in the same closet. This needs to be a covert operation, as most children do not understand why all of their papers are not kept.

Before Grace headed off to college, she went through each box and decided what she would want to keep longer term, so we consolidated significantly from more than a dozen letter-sized boxes down to one. It was her choice what she wanted to hold on to and look back at what she created as a child as she headed into adulthood.

My friend took a different approach. She basically saved everything until the end of the school year and then had her children choose which items they wanted to keep and which they wanted to pitch. At the end of the year, each child would have a letter-sized box that she would store away for them.

Art projects present a unique challenge, since your child will bring home a wide range of "art." So, decide what you want to keep and what is quietly "set aside" in the recycling bin.

Actually, many of the gifts Grace has given to her father for Father's Day or his birthday have been framed pieces of art she made at school, which helped to preserve some of the most special pieces she had created over the years.

REVIEWING REPORT CARDS

Due to the fact that schools generally send out grades electronically, we can all look at them without reviewing them together. It is important to create a moment when you reflect with your child in terms of how they are doing in school.

Throughout Grace's school years, we would sit down together with her when her report card came and discussed the details with her. This was always a great opportunity to understand how Grace was feeling about how she was doing in school and for us to reflect together on the fact that we were proud of her efforts as long as she was doing the best she could in her classes.

ATTENDING PARENT-TEACHER CONFERENCES

If possible, it is helpful for you and your spouse/partner to attend parent-teacher conferences together (even if you two are divorced), as this enables you to show to the teachers that both of you are involved in your children's lives.

We always attended Grace's parent-teacher conferences together. In fact, at Grace's school, she also attended the conferences (starting in middle school), so she was also able to see that we were both there for her and wanted to engage with her teachers on how she was doing in school.

FINDING THE RIGHT GUIDANCE FOR YOUR CHILD

It is inevitable that, during our children's lives, they will need some additional support when it comes to managing their academic world.

This can range from tutoring or academic support, to finding the best solution to manage ADHD or anxiety, to a myriad of other challenges that children face during their academic careers.

There is so much to think through in these instances... finding the best resources to help your child will always be your top priority, but it can sometimes be a challenge as you are managing the juggling act.

My friend shared that there is generally a parent (or two) in any given school who has focused their efforts on figuring out the best resources to address a specific topic. So, you need to work to find those individuals (sometimes through networking with other parents or through recommendations from your child's school) in order to ensure that you are engaging the best resources to help your child.

THE ENERGY BOOST
FROM GIVING BACK

With everything we try to squeeze into a given week or month, sometimes the idea of finding time to give back seems daunting (and exhausting) to even think where you will find the time to squeeze it in.

What I found over the years is that I had to be realistic about what I could expect to commit to when it came to truly giving back, as I did not want to commit to something and not be able to follow through with it.

So, I set up some parameters for what I would try to do when it came to giving back.

I would volunteer for only one of the school parties (and I chose Valentine's Day... and I will go into detail on this choice a little later).

I would volunteer for one other school-related activity that I could fit into my work schedule.

I would find one community volunteer activity that we (Grace and I) could do together (starting at age seven) and that could become a tradition for us in terms of serving our community together (and I will share a bit more about this later).

I would be on only one non-profit board.

This was all that I could handle in addition to raising Grace and my job, and I was okay with this being the case.

Now, there are so many ways to give back. If you have more time to give back to your children's school or to your community, then go for it. I wanted to focus on what I could truly commit to, whether it was at school or in the community. However, I also needed to figure out how to strike the right balance between the demands of being a working parent and the expectations of being a contributing member of the school community and our community as a whole.

SCHOOL VOLUNTEER EXPECTATIONS

The expectation of parental involvement varies based on the age of your children as well as the school they attend. Depending on the type of school your children go to, there can be significant expectations in terms of parental involvement in supporting the school (and this is beyond writing checks for fundraisers or endowments). This can range from volunteering in the school library to being present in the classroom for a range of activities and events.

It is important to understand what is expected of you as a parent in terms of participation within your children's school.

When we were looking at schools for Grace to attend after pre-school, there was a range of expectations, depending on the schools we were considering. One school explicitly stated that, if you could not volunteer in the school library throughout the year, it would be an issue. So, needless to say, this was not the school that Grace attended, as neither her father nor I was able to commit to this policy, given the demands of our jobs.

I will never forget when we went to the open house for the school we chose for Grace, and the kindergarten teacher said to us, "We will be teaching your children, and we do not expect you to be here in the classroom with us." I smiled at my husband and whispered to him, "This is the school for us."

The reason I chose to share this story is that you need to figure out what you are able and willing to take on when it comes to involvement in your children's school. It is a pressure that you can feel throughout their school career if you do not choose wisely in terms of whether the school will work for your children as well as for you as a working parent.

VOLUNTEERING AT SCHOOL

There are many different opportunities for you to volunteer at school, so you need to be selective, based on the time you can carve out of your work schedule for the specific volunteer activities. At a minimum, it is worth considering just picking one event at school to volunteer for and making it a tradition. If you are able to do more, then that's great... but if you have only limited time to carve out of your busy work schedule, then choose wisely, and make it memorable.

From my standpoint, I wanted to do one activity that would involve being in the classroom with Grace and her classmates, as it is fun to meet all of the children and see the dynamics between them at various ages.

So, I decided to sign up for the Valentine's Day party for a range of reasons. It is not during one of the other crazy times of the year (Halloween, Christmas, year-end). It is always a special day to celebrate, and I had an idea of what to bring that would be fun to do with Grace and easy to handle the night before the party.

The Valentine's Day Party tradition continued from age three, when Grace was in pre-school, through age ten, when she was in fifth grade (which was the last year they had these types of parties with parents involved).

We would make heart-shaped cut-out sugar cookies with homemade frosting and red Jello "knox blocks" in the shape of hearts (using the smaller heart-shaped cookie cutter so that they would be bite-sized).

If you do not know what Jello "knox blocks" are... they are basically jello mixed with extra gelatin so they stick together and can be cut out in any shape you want (see recipe in Appendix). You can cut them in squares, or you can use simple cookie cutters to cut them into shapes like hearts or stars. They are a huge hit with children of all ages and parents alike and became part of our Valentine's Day Party tradition.

A quick side note on homemade treats versus store-bought... both are going to be acceptable when you are involved in these classroom parties. I just enjoyed the activity of making these treats with Grace, and it was a fun part of the tradition for us each year.

I also protected Valentine's Day each year and made sure I could attend the party and help with anything else that was planned for the event by the other mothers who were involved.

Over the years, I would also look for other activities that enabled me to give back to Grace's school, while also giving back to the community (such as driving for the supply drive we held for shelters around the city). These types of activities did not necessarily involve Grace or her class directly but did allow me to get to know other parents at the school who were involved in these activities.

Again, I made an effort to protect the time on my calendar at work, so it was possible to stick to the commitment I had made to the school for these volunteer activities.

The key thing to take away from volunteering at school is to focus on what you can truly commit to at school and ensure that you deliver on what you signed up for, as the other parents and the children are depending on you.

VOLUNTEERING IN YOUR COMMUNITY

Even with all that we do on a daily basis in raising our children and focusing on our careers, one of the best things we can do is volunteering and performing acts of kindness for others. If possible, include your children in this with you.

One point to think through is how much time you truly have to give back while you are focused on raising your children, managing your career, and, potentially, already volunteering at your children's school.

If you think you have the capacity to do more, then I would recommend picking one volunteer organization and focusing your time on that organization.

I looked for a long time before finding the right organization for me to get involved with (beyond Grace's school), and I am so happy I waited until I found the right one.

The organization I chose to be involved with is a special organization called Jack and Jill Late Stage Cancer Foundation (JAJF). This organization sends families in which one of the parents is terminally ill with cancer on their last trip as a family. The oncologist treating the sick parent actually prescribes the trip. I have had the privilege of being on JAJF's Board of Advisors for many years, and the ability to provide whatever support I can to this special organization has been so fulfilling.

TEACHING YOUR CHILDREN ABOUT GIVING

One of the things that is important to fit into the juggling act is figuring out how to teach our children about giving to the community.

When they are young, it is hard to find opportunities to do so. One of the things we did was to give Grace three piggy banks... one for savings, one for spending, and one for giving. Each week, we gave her three dollars, and she had to put a dollar in each piggy bank.

Once she had enough money in her giving bank, then we let her pull it out and decide where she wanted to donate it. She wanted to give it to the Humane Society, due to her love of animals. So, we drove her to the Humane Society, and she gave them her donation. We thought this would be more powerful than us taking the money and writing a check and sending it in.

Once Grace was old enough to volunteer with me, we went to a local soup kitchen and served the homeless together. We did this from the time she was seven years old until eighteen, when she graduated from high school.

There were so many lessons that we took away each time we served together. There was a time when one of the homeless people being served tried to tip Grace as she was serving his table because he appreciated how she was approaching her role and wanted to thank her. She told him she could not take the tip but appreciated the sentiment. Grace and I talked about this on the drive home and reflected on the fact that the man barely had any money in his pockets but still felt compelled to share it with her.

These experiences can fill your spirit in a way that nothing else can... especially when you can all share in the important lessons from helping those who are in need.

My mom has had multiple careers... and each career has had a focus on improving other people's lives... she started out as a nurse, then she made a decision to stay home to raise me and my younger brothers... and while raising us she started a flower business for weddings which was an outlet for her creativity and love of flowers... although I think this might have been a strategy to have fresh flowers in the house at all times.

She also has had one "career" that has stretched over the past 45+ years... above and beyond being an incredibly supportive wife, mother, and grandmother (aka Gigi). My mom had a fabulous career, but the work she has done is generally not recognized as a "career"... I am referring to the hard work of volunteering, fund-raising, and planning events for multiple organizations in whichever city she is living in... she has always been incredibly giving of her time and energy.

This has been an inspiration to me in terms of her endless focus on giving back to others... and is one of the inspirations for me writing this book. I want to continue the tradition of giving back to others in the way my mom has done for so many years, but in my own unique way. Hopefully, this will also set an example for Grace that you can define your own path for giving back to your community based on what fulfills you.

THE STAYING POWER OF
FAMILY MEMORIES

When I reflect back on what I remember as a child, the memories that stand out and that I cherish are all related to the travel we did as a family, the traditions we followed as a family, and those special moments with one of my parents.

As I was raising Grace, I tried to use this as a guide when thinking about the experiences we were having together and the memories we were creating from those experiences.

There are many special moments from my childhood that make me smile. It will be interesting to see what Grace looks back on over the years in terms of the memories that stand out from her childhood. My hope is that the many special moments that we have had together over the years make her smile.

THE GIFT OF TRAVEL

I truly believe the best gift we can give our children is travel. Travel comes in all forms... from driving to the town, city, or state near where you live, to flying to visit a different region of the country, to traveling internationally.

Regardless of the actual destination, the ability to expose our children to different places enables them to experience new places that may (or may not) be like the place you live. Any and all exposure is a gift, as it helps to build our children's perspective on the world we live in.

A one-hour drive to a new place can be considered "travel" by children... the change in their environment is always a positive. It is fun to explore a new area of your city or state.

Take a bus, train, plane, or drive... it is the experience of going somewhere and exploring together that creates new and special memories with your children.

Personally, I have had the opportunity and privilege to travel to 46 out of 50 of the United States (just four more to go) as well as 55+ countries around the world (so far).

So, when it came to traveling with Grace, I first wanted to expose her to my favorite cities in the U.S. so she could appreciate the country we live in. We had a great time exploring a range of cities across the country, from Washington, DC, to New York City, to Chicago, to Seattle.

I always loved traveling with Grace, whether it was going to the beach and taking long walks and watching her chase the sandpipers or visiting the aquarium in the city we were visiting (we have been to many aquariums around the country due to Grace's love of marine life). Each time, we came away from those trips with special memories that we still remember fondly together.

WEEKEND TRAVEL

There is something about a weekend away that is so special, whether it is with your children exploring a new spot, with your spouse/partner for some much-needed time together, visiting family, with your girlfriends catching up, or even solo to spend some quality time with yourself. Whichever of the options you decide to do in any given year, ideally you are able to do a combination of these types of weekend trips.

When it comes to exposing your children to new places, I found that, with Grace, we could get the sense of the city over a two-day period. It was enough exposure for us to decide if it was a place that we would want to come back to someday.

An example of this is when I took Grace to Seattle and Vancouver for a summer vacation when she was twelve years old. We spent two days in Seattle before heading on to Vancouver. As we were exploring Seattle over the weekend, Grace said at one point, "Mom, this is my place," and I said, "Well, maybe you'll live here someday."

Based on that exposure, Grace decided she wanted to go to college in Seattle and focused her efforts on getting into the University of Washington and Seattle University. She was accepted at both schools and decided she wanted to go to Seattle University. I know that our trip together to Seattle had a significant impact on Grace's perspective on the city and ultimately helped to shape where she would go to college.

VACATIONS

There are various ways to think about the approach you take to a vacation when you are managing the juggling act of being a working parent.

There is the vacation that will give an experience to your children, which can be in the form of a sightseeing trip to Washington, DC, or a trip to Disney World. Regardless of the experience, it generally requires some upfront planning, and it can be a fun (and exhausting) trip for all involved. You will definitely create special memories with your children on these types of vacations.

There is the vacation when you visit family in a different location from where you live, which is always a special time for you and your children to spend time with family. However, it may not fully qualify as "a vacation," depending on what is entailed when visiting your family.

Last, but not least, is the vacation where you leave your children with a nanny/sitter, a family friend, or a family member, and you travel with your spouse/partner or with girlfriends to unplug from the juggling act. It is fair to say that the above two categories of giving your children an experience and visiting family are not necessarily the same thing as unplugging on a beach somewhere with a cocktail nearby, with no one to take care of and no family commitments that need to be taken into consideration.

If possible, try to fit the various types of vacation into a given year so that you can balance providing experiences and connecting with family while also recharging your own battery... so you can continue to manage the juggling act.

NOTE: A disclaimer about your first vacation as new parents. The first vacation can be beyond challenging... as you adjust to all of the gear you need to have, the change in routine for your children (including unfamiliar sleeping arrangements), etc. Unfortunately, these early vacations do not necessarily provide the recharging you need, so you need to change your expectations about what you are going to get out of a vacation when young children are part of the equation in the very early years. (See 'Traveling Tests' for more on this topic).

TRADITIONS

When it comes to traditions, there are traditions that you may want to pass on to your children from your own childhood, and there may be new traditions that you want to start as a family. Either way, the traditions that you stick to each year form a strong foundation of the memories that your children will remember well when they look back on their childhood.

As you start to reflect on the family traditions that you want to create, think about what is important to you and the moments you want to share with your children each year.

It is fun to think back on the traditions that we had as a family. I have highlighted one of my favorites in the "Holiday Traditions" section.

HOLIDAY TRADITIONS

Holidays… just the word can have working parents' hearts start to beat faster. From the extra things that take place at school around the holidays, to the extra things you need to think about at home in terms of decorating the house, to making or ordering costumes, to buying and wrapping gifts, to hiding Easter eggs.

The holidays are meant to be fun and special for you and your family, but they can feel stressful and overwhelming. So, my recommendation is to figure out what you truly want to include in your holiday traditions and just focus on those elements each year. The goal should be to keep each holiday at the lowest stress level possible (which, I realize, is easier said than done).

One of my favorite holiday traditions was that we made and delivered "mudballs" to our friends every Christmas. Just to clarify, a "mudball" is a small ball made up of peanut butter and Rice Krispies mixed together and then dipped in chocolate (see recipe in Appendix).

Grace was my "elf" and would help me make and package the mudballs each year, and then we would spend a Sunday after-noon delivering mudball packages to friends around the city.

Our mudballs became such an anticipated tradition during Christmas that, in some families, whoever was there when the mudballs were delivered did not tell the rest of the family right away, so that they could enjoy a few for themselves without having to share with the rest of the family. One friend always said, "The Christmas season is not official until your mudballs arrive."

We had so much fun delivering mudballs together each year, and it was quality time with Grace during the holidays, as we were spreading holiday cheer together.

Another aspect of holiday traditions is who you spend the holidays with as a family. Whether you live near your extended family or not can define what this looks like. We lived across the country from our family, so we spent certain holidays traveling to see family. Other holidays, we stayed home and either hosted friends or went over to friends' homes to celebrate. I refer to this as our "family of friends," and we were very fortunate to spend many special holidays with special friends who truly became like family to us.

BIRTHDAYS

As a working parent, there were some things that I still wanted to put extra effort into for Grace, and one of those things was her birthdays.

Each year we have a tradition in my family of making a home-made carrot cake for our birthdays, which is made in different shapes. So, over the years, I made Grace a butterfly, a teddy bear, a dinosaur, an iPod, a putting green (when she was playing golf), a rowing oar (when she was rowing crew), a sailboat (the year she learned to sail) and, of course, a car for her sixteenth birthday (very predictable). The fun part was that we made the cake together with my parents (to whom Grace refers as "Gigi and Papa"), who came into town each year to celebrate Grace's birthday. It was a very fun tradition for us to share together.

When Grace was young, she had an equal number of girlfriends and boyfriends, and, in her younger years, they all came to her birthday party together. However, at the age where sleepovers became an option, Grace would have a sleepover with her girlfriends at our house, but Grace still wanted to celebrate her birthday with her boyfriends. So, Grace's dad would take Grace and her boyfriends (six of them) out to dinner at a restaurant that Grace would choose. She would dress up, and she wanted the boys to be dressed in jackets (we lived in Atlanta at the time, so this was not completely out of the question for boys to do, without too much complaining). This was a birthday tradition for Grace from age seven to age twelve.

These birthday traditions make me smile when I think back on how we celebrated Grace's special day each year.

BIRTHDAY QUESTIONS LIST

A birthday tradition that I started when Grace was three years old is that I would ask her the same list of twenty-plus questions and keep them in the same file so we could see how she answered the questions (the same or differently) each year.

We would not show Grace the answers from the previous years. In some instances, her answers stayed the same for a number of years, and, in some instances, she would change her answer every year. Either way, it gave us fun insight into how Grace's perspective was evolving as she grew up.

The list of questions that I asked Grace each year on her birthday can be found in the Appendix.

MOVIE NIGHT TRADITION

After my divorce, one of my favorite traditions with Grace was our Friday evenings, which entailed ordering in sushi and watching movies together. We kept a running list of movies we wanted to watch. She exposed me to movies she thought I would like, and I exposed her to movies from my generation. We each had a fur throw, and we would curl up on the couch together and watch movies.

When it comes to planning fun traditions with your children, the traditions do not need to be extravagant. Sometimes the best traditions are the ones that are easiest to plan and truly maintain as a tradition over the years.

SPECIAL MOMENTS

Special moments are hard to plan... they just happen. When they do... take note, take a photo, or write down a quote or a snippet of what just happened that made it special, as these special moments can last a lifetime. They are the memories that you and your children will look back on with a smile.

I have vivid memories of the special moments from my own childhood, and they definitely stand out as memories that I cherish.

THE GIFT OF SPECIAL PHOTOS

One thing I invested in over the years was having Grace photographed by a professional photographer... this may seem like an extravagance, but I viewed it as a gift to myself. We took them every year around her birthday, and we were able to capture her growth throughout her life in classic black-and-white photos which I will always treasure.

We also used these photos for our annual holiday card and framed photos for grandparents as gifts for the holidays. So, these photos served many purposes each year and were well worth the investment.

I have some of my favorites of Grace framed in my home office, and they make me smile each time I look at them.

COOKING TOGETHER

As a working parent, dinner time can be a stressful part of the day, depending on how many you are cooking for and the varying degrees of tastes within your crew.

As Grace became old enough to help out in the kitchen, I asked her to join me in helping to prepare meals. It started with her making her own breakfast, and then we moved on to dinner.

When Grace showed an interest in cooking (in middle school), I asked her to research new recipes that she wanted to try. We had a list on our computer in the kitchen. Each Sunday night, we tried a new recipe, and Grace continued to expand her portfolio of recipes that she was excited to prepare for dinner. We even got to the stage where Grace was the one cooking, and I was her sous chef.

The irony is that, through making these dinners (and also cooking with her Dad at his place), Grace has become a much better cook than I am, and she has gained confidence that she can make whatever she wants, which is fun to see.

INSPIRATIONAL QUOTES BEFORE DINNER

We divorced when Grace was seven years old, and, at that point, I wanted to start a new tradition at dinnertime, since it would be just the two of us. A friend had given me a book of inspirational quotes during my divorce, so each night before dinner, we each read an inspirational quote and reflected on what we had just read. It was a special way to start our dinners together... and led to some interesting discussions.

Needless to say, over the years, we went through many books of inspirational quotes, but it was a special tradition we shared... and I look back on our dinners together, as well as the inspiration we took from those quotes, with a smile.

FUN WITH MUSIC PLAYLISTS

There is some irony in me writing on this topic because I am one of those people who can never remember the name of the artist or the name of the song. However, I am surrounded by people who love music and are well-versed in these details. So, I wanted to call out that one of the things that I have enjoyed doing as a parent with Grace is putting together playlists that we would enjoy listening to together.

It started in the early days of driving her carpool, and it continued as I asked Grace to make me playlists for my birthday or Christmas gifts (much easier and more thoughtful than a store-bought gift). She made me a playlist for working out and a playlist for relaxing. These lists were always a mix of my favorite songs and songs that Grace thought I would like from her own list of favorites. These are still the playlists that I listen to most often because they make me smile knowing that she made them for me.

PARENTING PHILOSOPHY
&
ESSENTIALS

As you become a parent and reflect on the type of parent you want to be, think about some of the philosophies that will guide your parenting approach.

For example, it definitely takes a village to raise children these days. So, we were always open to other influences on Grace as a child, which included nannies, teachers, friends, and family.

When we had Grace, we also made the decision that she would fit into our life and that we would not completely change everything due to her presence. In the very early days of her life, there were many nights when Grace was in her baby carrier under the table while her father and I enjoyed dinner at our favorite restaurant.

I cannot stress enough the importance of teaching independence to our children, so their wings can be strong and fly when they need to (which is covered in the following section).

These are just a few examples of the different philosophies that we embraced as we raised Grace. You have already seen a number of these philosophies throughout the book, and there are more reflected in this section.

Take some time to reflect on the parenting philosophies that are important to you, and define those that will be a north star as you go along your parenting journey.

SPENDING QUALITY TIME
WITH YOUR CHILDREN

The reality is that, when you are trying to manage the juggling act of life, it can be a challenge to give your children the focused attention they need and deserve.

Focus on spending quality time with your children. How you define "quality time" will depend on the age of your children.

Try to make a conscious effort to be present with your children when you are spending time with them. This may be easier said than done, but it will ensure that you stay connected to your children and how they are doing.

It can be a challenge, given the long list of things you are most likely juggling on a day-to-day basis. So, this may entail carving out specific times during when you "power down"... put away your laptop, mobile phone, or "To Do" list... whatever is distracting you... and focus on engaging with your children.

This can be spending time discussing their day over dinner, walking the dog together, or just hanging out on the couch, watching one of their favorite programs together (but not multitasking at the same time).

Throughout this book, I have mentioned various bits of advice on how to protect the time you have with your children. If you work on adopting the collective guidance, I truly think it can have a significant impact on the time you are spending with your children when you are not working to ensure that your time together is quality time.

TEACHING INDEPENDENCE

We also have raised Grace to be as independent as possible, as early as possible. We wanted her wings to grow strong, so that, when she headed off to college, she would have the strength to fly wherever she wanted to go (versus clipping her wings and requiring her to stay close to home).

This independence can be in the form of making decisions for themselves, cooking, household chores (e.g., laundry and cleaning), understanding how to pay bills and file insurance forms, or traveling on a plane solo. There are many moments when we can teach our children the power of independence and the importance of being able to do things for themselves. This is a gift you can give your children, but it is also a muscle which needs to be built.

The ability and confidence to be independent is learned over time. Some children are wired to be both confident and independent, and others need to be shown what it looks and feels like to take responsibility for themselves. Empowering our children to be independent is the greatest gift we can give them because it gives them the autonomy they need to go out into the world and lead a healthy and happy life.

THE BALANCING ACT OF CO-PARENTING

Whether you are married or divorced, there is a balancing act of co-parenting with your spouse/partner, or ex-spouse that requires communication, coordination, and patience. There are many things to manage when you are parenting your children, and if you are both focused on your career at the same time, then the balancing act is very real.

The level of engagement of your spouse/partner or ex-spouse will also define what the balancing act looks like between the two of you as you manage the logistics of life from a parenting standpoint.

Also, when it comes to decisions you make jointly about raising your children, always try to back each other up. This is an important principle to align on, as children can try to play one parent off of the other. So, agreeing that you will always try to back each other up is a great starting point for the approach you will take to co-parenting.

I was fortunate that my husband, later ex-husband, was very engaged in raising our daughter. We were aligned on the approach we wanted to take (both when we were married and when we were divorced), which made the balancing act easier to manage. It still required clear communication, careful coordination, and patience (from both of us).

ABSENT CO-PARENT

If you are married, there can be instances when your spouse/ partner is "absent," and you feel like you are a single parent.

This can be a challenging dynamic to manage, depending on the situation.

If there is a specific reason that your spouse/partner is not able to be present in your children's lives and it is unavoidable, then you need to do what you can to ensure your children feel loved and supported, even though one of their parents is not actively involved in raising them.

If you are in a scenario in which your spouse/partner is capable of being more present but is choosing not to be active in your children's lives, then this is a situation where you need to decide how you discuss this with your spouse/partner. Explain that this is not a sustainable model for raising your children and that you expect them to play a more active role in your children's lives.

TRUE CONFESSIONS

Depending on your child, the thoughts they want to share come out during the day-to-day routines of life... during car-pool, during bath time or tucking them into bed when they are young.

Sometimes it is when you are most tired that your children open up and share what is truly going on in their heads. It is those moments that you need to try to pause and take it all in... because these moments are a window that is not always open, and these are special times when your children are sharing something they want you to know.

As a working parent, sometimes it can be easy for you to become distracted or not fully present during these moments. Do what you can to be fully present, so that, when those confessions of what your child is truly thinking are shared, you are hearing what they are sharing with you and taking in that special or important reflection.

BEDTIME ROUTINES

As a working parent, one of the things I tried to protect was being around for bedtime (except for those times when I was traveling or out to dinner).

I loved this part of our evening. When Grace was little, we would sit in a big overstuffed chair in the corner of her room and read books together... and, as she got older, I would relax in the chair, and Grace would flop on her bed while we would talk about all sorts of topics.

Even when Grace was in her high-school years, I always made it a point to go up to her room and kiss her goodnight before she went to sleep. She was old enough to not necessarily need me to do this, but it was a special moment when I could say "I love you" to her at the end of the day.

SECURE BACK-UP FOR SPECIAL ITEMS

When your children are young, they may become attached to a special item... a stuffed animal, a blanket or something else. If this is the case, then I would advise buying a second, back-up of the specific item to store away in case the first one is lost... or becomes worn out and not usable.

Grace became attached to a specific white blanket that had been given to me by a friend when she was born. Once it looked like this was going to be her "blankie" for the long term, I decided to hunt down a second one to have just in case. This ended up being a good call because there was a point where the first blanket was so tattered and torn (as it was a delicate knit and not meant to be washed as much as it was)... and having the second blanket to pull out and use a couple of years into her attachment to this special item was helpful.

One of my favorite examples of this is when my friend's three year old daughter had a special stuffed animal named, Owlie, which was well-loved. Her daughter asked her to take Owlie on a business trip to NYC with her, so she just put it into her tote bag. There was a point where my friend realized that Owlie had fallen out of her tote. She tried to retrace her steps to find Owlie in NYC, but with no luck.

My friend had the foresight due to her daughter's attachment and had actually already purchased a back-up for Owlie. So, when she got home she pulled out the back-up and gave it to her daughter. Her daughter asked what happened to

Owlie because she was so fluffy... and my friend said that Owlie had gone to the "fluff-up spa" in NYC. Needless to say, we had a good laugh as my friend shared this story and was another reminder that having a back-up for special items is a good strategy.

HELPING YOUR CHILDREN WITH GIFT GIVING

There will be several times during the year when you will need to think through how you want to handle helping your children pick out and pay for gifts for the other parent (for birthday, holidays, etc.).

There are a number of ways you can handle this:

- ~ Help your children with thinking through gift ideas, with purchasing the gifts, and with wrapping the gifts (with your children helping with the gift wrapping, regardless of age).

- ~ Delegate to your nanny or another family member helping your children with the purchasing and the wrapping of gifts.

- ~ Leave it to your children to figure it out (depending on the age of the children, this may be an option).

Regardless of which option you choose, the most important point is to help your children feel good about how they are recognizing the other parent for the special occasion... teach them the valuable lesson of giving gifts (versus receiving).

This, hopefully, will ensure that you do not go through a birthday or holiday without any special recognition from your children.

Actually, I have always told Grace that she does not need to buy me a gift but that I would like her to be thoughtful when it comes to figuring out a gift to give me for a special occasion. For example, she has made me coupons for movie nights at the house, a coupon for "tech support" (since I can be technologically challenged at times), a playlist of her favorite songs, or a promise to go on long walks in the neighborhood together. I would much prefer to have these types of gifts or a thoughtfully written card from Grace than anything she could ever buy for me.

THREE PIGGY BANKS

As I mentioned earlier, starting at age three, we paid Grace an allowance. At the time, we set up three piggy banks... one for saving, one for spending, and one for giving. Whenever Grace received her allowance, she needed to split it across the three piggy banks. We wanted to teach her that she needs to think about these three areas of financial consideration as she grows older.

In addition, in the approach to giving I referenced earlier, the focus on saving money you earned was something that my parents instilled in me at a young age, so I also wanted to pass this on to Grace.

When I was a teen, my parents said that if I made any money outside of the house, they would match any money that I deposited into my savings account. This was definitely a motivator for me. So, we did the same thing for Grace when she was growing up. Any money that she made outside of the house or pulled out of her savings piggy bank and deposited into the bank, we matched.

There is so much written about helping your children learn about finances. From my experience, the simple action of the three piggy banks and the matching principle really helped to reinforce certain basic financial principles.

THE SPIRITUAL SIDE OF THINGS

There is so much that could be written about how you manage the spiritual side of your life both as an individual and as a parent raising your children.

Spirituality means different things to different people, so I am not going to go in depth on this topic in this book.

However, I will share that we focused on ensuring that we instilled a strong base of values in Grace throughout her childhood… such as compassion, honesty, curiosity, optimism, respect, trustworthiness… the list goes on.

Grace was raised Catholic, and she was baptized and confirmed in the Catholic Church. She went to Sunday school throughout grade school and then attended a Catholic Youth Group each Sunday throughout middle school and high school. Through this exposure, she built upon the strong set of values we were instilling in her at home.

Regardless of the approach you take to your own spirituality and how you approach teaching spirituality to your children (if this is something you choose to do), it is important to model the values you want your children to adopt by how you approach your day-to-day life. Our children are watching us each day, and the way we live our values is one of the best lessons we can provide to our children. They will carry these lessons with them throughout their lives.

THERAPY FOR YOUR CHILDREN

There may be phases in your children's lives when they need some extra support beyond what they receive from you and/or your spouse/partner, siblings, extended family, teachers, coaches, and any other special people in their lives.

During these phases, it is worthwhile to explore whether to engage a therapist to help your child through the phase for a short or extended period of time. It is helpful for our children to understand at a young age that therapy is a viable and acceptable tool to use when needed and that it is not taboo to see a therapist to help us think through challenges we may be facing in life.

DISCIPLINING YOUR CHILDREN

If and when there is a need to discipline your children, there needs to be an aligned approach to it between parents. Otherwise, it will not be feasible to reinforce the change in behavior you are looking for from your children.

Whether the discipline includes reduced screen time, a phone or car being taken away for a period of time, or being grounded and not able to be involved in social events with friends, you and your spouse/partner's united front is the most important part.

MONITORING SCREEN TIME

The approach you and your spouse/partner take to monitoring screen time for your children is also a point you should align on in order to be as consistent as possible.

For example, you need to consistently reinforce if there is a time limit to "screen time" for your children (on the computer, mobile phone, social media, or gaming). If you are not consistent, then this can be both confusing for the children and challenging for the parent who has tried to place limitations on screen time.

As parents in this digital age, we are all trying to figure out the balance of what is acceptable and appropriate for our children in terms of how much screen time they are allowed. Figuring out the right approach to managing this aspect of your children's lives is not an easy part of parenting.

However, there should be a conscious decision on how you want to monitor what your kids are doing, as it will be one of the most important things you can do as a parent as technology becomes an influence on your children's lives.

The topic of the impact of technology (including social media) on our children could fill an entire book (and there are plenty of books that you can read on this topic). So, I am going to pass on providing any further guidance on this topic, as I think there are other sources to guide you on all that is entailed in being a parent in this technology-focused (and social media influenced) age we are living in.

My only advice is to think about how your use of technology is being observed by your children, as this does define the expectations they have of how technology integrates into their lives as well.

RULES OF ENGAGEMENT FOR MOBILE PHONES

There are a number of points to think through and align on when it comes to mobile phones.

The first is at what age your children are allowed to get a mobile phone. This is a decision both parents should make together.

Also, if there are certain rules that you want to have your children agree to in terms of mobile-phone usage, then you and your spouse/partner should agree on these points with your children to ensure there will be consistency in what is allowed (and not allowed).

We actually asked Grace to write a mobile-phone contract that outlined the rules of engagement relating to use of her mobile phone. We wanted to ensure that Grace fully understood that having a mobile phone is a responsibility and a privilege, not a given.

THE TEST OF DRIVING

When you get to the stage when your children are getting their driver's license, it will be a moment that comes with a range of emotions.

I will never forget the day I watched Grace drive off on her own in a car... it was a moment of pride (for her), a feeling of freedom (for both of us). It was also a moment when I had to figure out what I needed to do to ensure that she stayed safe as she was heading out into the world.

A friend recommended getting an app that allows you to understand where your children are in the car they are driving in. Some of the apps also let you know how fast they are driving, which can be a helpful point of reference if you are concerned that your child likes to test the boundaries of speed limits.

This is a milestone in life that requires us as parents to figure out how we are now meant to parent with this new dynamic in our lives.

However, I must admit that I was very happy that Grace was able to get her license and get where she needed to go on a daily basis. It opened up time in my schedule that I had not had to play with in many years and allowed me to think about how I wanted to use the gift of time I had just been given each week.

CONNECTING WITH OTHER PARENTS

As your children start to have more freedom with driving themselves around, it is important to be in communication with the parents of the other children your child is spending time with... and staying on top of what they are doing.

Keeping our children safe is the number-one priority, so comparing notes with other parents is highly recommended.

CHILDREN DATING

If your children are in or heading into the teen years, then you will want to ensure that you discuss with your spouse/partner how you want to handle your children's dating activities. This can range from how to handle group dating to chaperoning, curfews, etc.

Once you two are aligned, then sit down with your children to discuss expectations, and ensure that they understand the rules of the road when it comes to dating while living in your house.

THE GIFT AND CHALLENGE OF BUSINESS TRAVEL

I must admit that I loved my business travel for a range of reasons, but the primary reason was that I was able to see the world and make a family of friends around the world... which was truly a gift.

There are also the challenges of business travel... you may miss a special moment of development for your child or an event at school, and those are moments when you would prefer to be home and be able to have that experience with your children.

The only advice I can give to parents who travel often for work is to try to make the coming and going from your travels as routine as possible with your children, so it does not end up being a traumatic experience each time you travel for work.

I completely appreciate that this is easier said than done, depending on the ages of your children and how they adjust during these moments of transition. However, I do think that the earlier that you travel in your children's lives, the more adjusted they will be over the course of their childhood for your coming and going as needed.

TAKE A MOMENT
TO REFLECT...

PRIORITIZING SELF-CARE TO STAY HEALTHY

It is up to you to determine what you want to focus on to help you feel good as you become a working parent and embark on this significant change in your life.

There are a range of things that you can do to ensure that you stay healthy, starting with prioritizing self-care, which includes getting enough sleep, working out, and taking time for yourself, away from your children.

These are not "optional" things that you can put at the bottom of your list. They are "must-do's" to ensure you stay healthy and happy as a working parent.

For many, taking care of oneself goes to the bottom of the list once you become a working parent.

We focus on taking care of our children, our spouses/partners, our homes, our jobs... we become conditioned to self-sacrifice versus self-care and putting everyone's needs before our own.

It is important to allow yourself the time you need to take care of yourself and the essential aspects of your life. This is easier said than done, because being a working parent is truly a juggling act. However, this is essential because your children deserve to have a healthy parent who has the energy to engage with them in a positive way.

RECHARGE YOUR BATTERY

Over the years, I have had a number of friends who have shared that they have not been away from their children for more than a couple of nights (even just one night) during their childhood.

Admittedly, I am going to sound very opinionated with this statement, but it comes from a place of love (and maybe a bit of tough love). It is important for you to be able to go away for a night, a weekend, or even a week without your children. Ideally, you would do this starting at a young age, so it is viewed as a normal occurrence for your children.

From my experience (and this is due to my career) I was traveling internationally from the time Grace was four months old. In some instances, she would stay with her father and, in some instances, our nanny (if both of us were going to be out of town). There were also times when my parents would come into town to stay with her.

Regardless of the situation, Grace knew from a very young age that Mommy goes on trips and that Mommy comes back from her trips. There were never any tears when I left, and there were always smiles when I arrived home. I attribute this dynamic to Grace becoming very used to her mother and father traveling for work as well as for vacations (weekends or longer) and that it was just part of our normal way of life.

I fundamentally believe that, in order to manage the juggling act of being a working parent, you need a break from your children and have some special time for yourself to recharge.

KEEPING AN EYE ON YOUR STRESS LEVEL

As you begin to juggle family and work commitments, it can become a stressful phase of your life, so try to ensure that you are watching out for any negative physical implications due to the increased stress in your life, whether it is losing too much weight or gaining too much weight, or any other type of stress-related ailment.

We cannot underestimate the impact stress can have on our bodies, so if you are feeling that the stress is having a negative impact on your health, please take the time to see your doctor and think through with them how you can manage your health effectively as you are managing the stress of being a working parent.

One of the best stress relievers I have found is to take long walks... just put on your running shoes and walk. This is good for both your mind and body.

PROTECT YOUR DOCTOR APPOINTMENTS

This is fundamental, so please repeat after me: "I will not reschedule my own doctor appointments."

Okay, so now that we are clear on that commitment you are making to yourself, please try to hold yourself to it.

Speaking from experience during my early years of being a working parent, I would constantly shift my doctor appointments due to work commitments and prioritize only Grace's appointments.

Now, it is important to ensure that your children have their regular doctor and dentist appointments, but it is equally important for your children's parents to have their appointments as well. We seem to somehow think these appointments are optional... and they are not. I cannot stress enough how important it is for you to keep these appointments in order to ensure that you can stay healthy for the long term.

SQUEEZING IN A WORKOUT

If there is one thing that can easily go by the wayside for you as a working parent, it is finding time to work out, which is a bummer.

So, do what you can to carve out the time to squeeze in a workout as many times a week that you can do it.

When you are trying to find out if you have time to work out (depending on your children's age), you may be able to have them join you, whether it is having your toddler in the jog stroller as you get in your walk or run, or having your pre-teen or teenager join you for a workout class.

There was a point where I was going to Pilates, and Grace would go with me and wait while I did my session. I finally decided she was old enough to try it, so instead of sitting reading a book and waiting for Mom, she joined me in the sessions. It was so fun to do those Pilates sessions with her over the years.

There also will be times when finding any time to work out is not feasible for parents with young children. During these periods, find ways to be active in your day-to-day routines to get your body moving (e.g., take the stairs whenever possible, or walk with your children somewhere versus taking the car). In these instances, it may not be the quickest way to get where you are going, but at least you are getting some type of exercise.

THE IMPORTANCE OF SLEEP

Sleep deprivation as a working parent is very real... and it is a problem for many working parents.

My biggest challenge as a working parent was getting enough sleep... and it is not because I don't like to sleep or can't go to sleep. It is because I always tried to pack too much into any given day, and the thing that suffered was my sleep.

If there is one thing I wish I could turn back the clock and change about my years of managing the juggling act would be to figure out how to get an hour of extra sleep each night.

I truly believe this is one of the most important things we can do for ourselves, and it makes such a difference in how we manage the juggling act each day.

DEALING WITH TIMES
OF EXHAUSTION

Regardless of what you are doing to manage the juggling act and be all things to all people in your life, there are times that you feel complete exhaustion... all you want to do is crawl into bed and sleep for twelve hours straight.

In these moments, when you think to yourself, "I am not sure I can get through this day," try to think about the things that might help you get through these periods, and identify some energy boosts that can help. These energy boosts are personal because what one person may find gives them energy, another person may view as an energy drain.

Energy boosts can range from the obvious such as a coffee or a little something sweet to making a phone call to your most-positive, energy-giving friend, to a hot shower at the end of the day... whatever can help you to get through that period of exhaustion until you can get that good night's sleep your body is needing.

Just spend a couple of moments thinking about what those energy boosts would be for you... and have them ready to trigger when those times of exhaustion hit you.

MANAGING YOUR ENERGY

There has been a lot written about the topic of managing your energy. I am a big believer in the fact that we need to focus on how we are managing our energy if we are going to try to accomplish all that we try to do in a given day as working parents.

Think about what gives you energy and what drains your energy... and these are very personal reflections. The day-to-day juggling act of a working parent requires energy. If you are being depleted of your energy on any given day, then you need to think about what your interaction needs to be with that person, event, or dynamic that is draining your energy. In some instances, we are not able to avoid these interactions, but if you can minimize them as much as possible, it can make a difference for your overall energy level.

Take the time to reflect on the energy givers and energy takers in your day-to-day life and try to minimize the energy takers having an impact on your life.

PRIORITIZE SELF CARE TO STAY HEALTHY

FIND YOUR SOUNDING BOARD

As you are managing the juggling act, it can be helpful to have someone to talk to if there are any specific challenges you are facing in your day-to-day life.

This can be a trusted friend you can walk and talk with… someone you can vent to about work, relationships, your children, etc. They need to be a good listener and someone who understands discretion/privacy.

It can also be worthwhile to find the right therapist, one who is able to help you think through the things you need to think through, listen when you need them to listen, and push you a bit when you need a little nudge if you are getting stuck on something that needs to be worked through.

It is worth noting that there is also a difference between trying to get advice from your friends and going to a professional therapist. There are times when a professional perspective is needed, so don't be shy about seeking out this type of professional help if it is needed. There are a range of sources for finding a great therapist, from word of mouth to online references. If you are needing some help thinking through things, then take the time to find the right therapist for you.

CLEAN OUT THE CLUTTER

As a working parent, there is a need to carve out some time each year to take stock of things in your home and clean out the clutter.

There is a balancing act when it comes to cleaning out the clutter in terms of keeping the things you may need and getting rid of those things that are just taking up space.

Whenever you take time to clean out the clutter, it is definitely therapeutic, and it can feel like you have lifted a weight off you.

A friend shared that, each year around birthdays and gift giving holidays, she and her children would clean out the toys together. The children would choose what they no longer had interest in and what they still loved. There was never a "getting-rid-of" quota, and, if they were undecided, they kept that item for another year.

This may not work for all children, but if you and your children can do this... it can help with managing the inevitable toy clutter that becomes part of your reality.

This approach is also age dependent. When your children are very young and are being inundated with toys, then put a portion of your children's toys away and pull them out down the road. This enables your children to enjoy the toys they have and then have "new" toys to play with when they need new stimulation.

There is also the need to set aside time each season to clean out your children's clothes… especially as they are growing so fast in their younger years.

If you have multiple children and want to put aside clothes you want to pass down, then figure out a storage game plan until you need them again. If you do not have the need to pass them down within your family, then think about who could use them. I had a close friend whose daughter was a year behind Grace, and we would give a large portion of the clothes she had outgrown for her daughter to enjoy.

Whatever the situation, once the season changes, there is no reason to keep winter or summer clothes which will not fit the following year in your child's closet or dresser. So, take the time to figure out where these clothes can go to avoid digging past the out-of-season or outgrown clothes to find what fits your child.

MANAGING TRANSITIONS

There are various transitions that can take place throughout the course of your journey as a working parent... including coming back from maternity/paternity leave, transitioning to having your next child, the adjustments that can come with raising multiple children and working, and adjusting to having an empty nest.

With each transition, there are considerations for you to think through, and we all navigate these transitions in different ways. There are no right or wrong ways to handle these transitions, but these are moments in time to reflect on how you want to manage the specific transition you are going through as part of your juggling act.

MATERNITY / PATERNITY LEAVE

It is always a question about how to approach going out for maternity/paternity leave and how to ramp back up after your leave. This is another personal decision in terms of what works best for you and your family.

It is important to know what you are entitled to when it comes to maternity/paternity leave based on your company's benefits plan. Then, state your intent. "I'm going out on leave. I will be back in X months, and I will prepare my coverage plan and work with you on my re-entry when it is time."

When the time comes, try to unplug when you are out on maternity/paternity leave, so you can truly focus on your new little one. It is a challenge to try to stay connected and to disconnect. Both approaches have pros and cons. However, unless you are running your own business and you are the only one that keeps things moving for your business, then it is worthwhile to try to completely disconnect and enjoy this special time with your family.

FIRST-TIME PARENT VERSUS HAVING 2+

My friends who had two or more children shared their reflections, since I cannot speak from this experience.

My friend shared that having the second one is both easier and harder for all of the obvious reasons. Each child brings new joy, trouble, work, and complexity.

One piece of advice is to incorporate the older child (children) into the new-baby experience as much as possible. Depending on the age of your first child, young children love being a "helper." They can "help" bathe their sibling, change their diapers, and put them down for a nap.

Try to make them feel like they are an important part of the baby-care process, so they do not feel shortchanged with the new resident in your house.

My friend can still envision her young daughter at the changing table on her stepstool, handing her the next needed item. She is sure that, at the time, her daughter thought her mom could not change a diaper without her.

I truly respect those working parents who are juggling multiple children and a career... as the juggling act becomes even more complicated when you add more children to the mix. Also, I want to recognize that there are many books on how to parent multiple children, so I will leave it to these books to go deep on this topic.

STRIVING FOR BALANCE
DURING A DIVORCE

If you are already a working parent, then you potentially have more flexibility in many of the topics that have been covered so far, such as what to do with the house and childcare, but the one thing you cannot do is be in two places at the same time.

My one bit of advice for working parents who are going through a divorce is to start to live the balance you need leading up to and through divorce... do not wait until you are officially divorced. The reason this is important is that there is conditioning that needs to take place for you, for your children, and for your workplace in terms of how you will be operating as you move forward. It is important to take into account the fact that you will not have another parent at home for backup on a day-to-day basis.

It is actually no different than when you had your first child. My advice to first-time moms is to start living your "working mom" schedule while you are pregnant, so you condition yourself to manage the various aspects of your life. Going through a divorce can be an adjustment similar to having your first child. It is a significant life event that requires you to reflect on all aspects of your life and to think through the changes that will be required on a day-to-day basis.

Ensure that you bring your boss and potentially a small group of colleagues into the loop as soon as you can, because there is potential to underestimate the time entailed in going through each step of the divorce process.

There will be times you will need to be out of the office for various meetings required for the process.

However, keep the circle small in terms of those individuals at work who know that you are going through a divorce, as your personal life should not become part of the hallway chatter.

Also, consider how much travel you are able and willing to do, given your new arrangement from a custody standpoint and the timeframe for your business travel. There may be certain nights you may not be able to go to a business dinner because you have your children. These dynamics need to be managed to ensure that you can deliver on what you need to do from a career standpoint, while also spending the time you need to with your children, especially as you are transitioning into this new way of living as a family.

Just try to be realistic as you work to balance the needs of your family and your career when you go through your divorce. It takes time to figure out the day-to-day juggling act of being a single working parent and what will work best for you and your children.

WHEN THE NEST IS EMPTY

When you are preparing for your children to head off to college or out into the world as a young adult, imagine yourself writing the next chapter of your life. Spend time thinking through what the new chapter title is going to be and what that chapter will entail.

This is a time of exploration and evolution. Take the opportunity to reflect on how you want to live your life in this next phase. You are still a parent, but you also have more freedom in your day-to-day life to do what you want with your time... and this time is a gift. This is a very personal reflection. It can be an exciting time to think about exploring the possibilities of what you want from your life as you start a new phase of life.

It is also okay to cry and mourn the end of an era. There is a wide range of emotions you may feel during this time, but just remember that your job as a parent is not done in this new phase of life.

The role you play in your child's life shifts to a different gear, and the "parenting" you do will entail providing guidance on topics like how to look for an apartment or how to manage a rental lease. Whatever the topic, the rewarding part of this phase of life is that your children are still looking for guidance, while they are learning what it means to start "adulting."

TAKE A MOMENT
TO REFLECT...

CAREER REFLECTIONS

As I was writing this book, it occurred to me that it might be helpful to share some of the reflections I have from my career. So, view this as an added bonus... and if this is not of interest, then you can skip this section.

Over the course of time, one of the things I have done is note down principles that have guided my career and kept me grounded and focused. I hope they can be of use to you in your own career journey.

As you go through life, it can be helpful to clearly outline both your personal and professional principles.

Reflecting back on my life, these are some things I wish someone would have said to me during college as I was trying to figure out what I was going to do with my life after being a student-athlete for so many years.

As a student-athlete, I was fortunate to focus every day on doing something that I love. I look back at the time I spent each day training for volleyball in the gym, weight room, and training room and think that I would not trade those times for anything. It was truly an amazing time in my life.

The challenge I had after graduating was to determine what I wanted to do after competing at a Division I level in a sport I loved. What should I focus my time, energy, and passion on moving forward?

I have to admit that, during my college years, I was so focused on balancing school, athletics, and a social life that I did not spend a great deal of time thinking about this question. I was enjoying the present but was not too concerned about the future.

Over the past thirty years, I have learned a great deal, so I wanted to share my reflections because I am still learning every day, and hopefully these points will be helpful as you think about your own life and career.

DEFINE WHAT MAKES YOU HAPPY EACH DAY

I am very clear on what makes me happy each day from a professional and personal standpoint.

From a professional standpoint, on an annual basis, I do a little mental check to see if my "criteria for happiness" are still being met. If not, then it is time to make a change. The criteria I have set for myself are pretty simple and straightforward:

- ~ Am I contributing?

- ~ Am I learning?

- ~ Am I being challenged?

- ~ Do I enjoy who I work with?

- ~ Am I compensated fairly?

- ~ Do I have the opportunity to travel the world?

- ~ Can I achieve a balance between family and work life, and is it working for both my family and me?

If any of these questions cannot be answered in a positive manner, then I need to reflect on whether I am in the right role... one that enables me to be as happy as possible in my career.

There may be times in life when you have something going on in your personal life that impacts your motivation to learn or be challenged in your work. It may be that you are just trying to put one foot in front of the other. If this is the case, then take this into consideration as you are trying to assess how you are feeling about your role. It may not be the best time to reflect on these questions and think through how "happy" you are from a professional standpoint.

ENJOY WHAT YOU DO…
DO WHAT YOU LOVE

You do not know what the future holds, so ensure that you enjoy each day and do what you love.

This may seem like a given… "Of course, I am going to enjoy what I do. Of course, I am going to do what I love." However, it is amazing how these two very important elements of your life can be lost over time. I cannot explain how this happens or why this happens, but I can say that there are quite a few people in this world… very bright, very successful people… who stop at some point in their lives and say, "I do not enjoy what I do."

The good news is that, if you define what makes you happy each day and you make conscious decisions to do what you love, then the scenario I just mentioned will not be one you live through… it is up to you.

The question I always ask someone who is evaluating their career path, usually new graduates or those looking to make a career pivot, is…

~ "What do you want to talk about every day?"

This seems like a basic question, but it is one that many people do not reflect upon enough when they are defining their career path.

It is also important to remember that you will eventually spend what you make, so do what you love.

This was actually great advice I was given when I was debating my very first job offer after college. One of the positions I was offered was for considerably more money than the other, but I was more interested in the lower-paying job. My boyfriend at the time said to me, "Take the job where you think you will be happiest. You will end up spending whatever you make." He was right.

BE CONSCIOUS OF THE PATH YOU ARE CHOOSING

Each decision you make in life takes you down a path with more decisions to make. The more questions you ask along the way and the more you understand, the better decisions you will make.

Throughout life, ask people what they do and how they decided to go in that direction. It is fascinating to learn the different paths people take. When you arrive at a state of reflection about your own career, it can help you think about your own path.

The "fork in the road" is our chance to make decisions, to make changes, to experiment with new possibilities. When you reach this fork, take risks... do not live life regretting your decisions. Remind yourself that you made the best decision for you at the time.

By the way, if you would have told me in 1993, as I was graduating from Georgetown, that, over the next thirty years, I would work for The Coca-Cola Company, McKinsey, and Google, traveling the world, visiting 55+ countries... I would have said, "You are crazy." I could not have imagined the amazing career and life experiences that I have been fortunate to have over the years. It is amazing to see how the decisions we make at each "fork in the road" impact our lives.

RECOGNIZE YOUR SKILLS

As a student-athlete, there are many skills I developed over the years that I may have taken for granted... the ability to manage my schedule so I can fit everything I want to do into a 24-hour day, the ability to build relationships with coaches and team members in order to achieve a common goal, or the ability to receive constructive feedback in order to continuously improve how I approach things... the list goes on and on.

There is one interesting skill I built as a student-athlete that I have underestimated over the years... I did not necessarily consider it a skill until I was traveling the world for my career. It's the ability to travel long distances and then perform at a high energy level.

When I fly for eighteen hours to Asia, the Middle East, or Africa, and then arrive at my destination and head into the office, this is really no different than a twelve-hour bus ride from Washington, DC, to Boston, and getting off the bus and onto the court to practice in order to get ready for a match.

There have been times during my career when people looked at me like I was crazy when I explained my travel schedule, and I would think to myself, "You have no idea how comfortable it is to work and sleep in a business class seat on an airplane versus trying to work and sleep on a Greyhound bus with a team of twelve girls, two coaches, and a trainer."

REFLECT ON WHAT YOU WANT TO BE KNOWN FOR

As you go through your career, reflecting on the question "What do you want to be known for?" is an interesting one to think through. There are many ways you could interpret this question...

- ~ How you show up as a leader

- ~ How you show up for your team

- ~ How you show up for your peers

- ~ The expertise and experience you bring to your work

Whichever angle you look to answer this question from, this can be a "north star" type of question to reflect on over time. It can guide how you interact with those around you... it can guide the type of work you focus on and the type of work you say "No" to throughout your career.

FIND A MENTOR

As a student-athlete, I was coached and mentored for most of my life due to my involvement in athletics. However, in the post-college world, coaches and mentors are not necessarily a given. I needed to seek them out and actively cultivate this relationship.

I have been very fortunate to have had mentors throughout different phases of my life. Each mentor has provided valuable guidance to me, and I will never forget the impact they have had on my life.

I am now at a stage in my career where I am actually mentoring a wide range of people of all ages around the world as they think about the various paths they can take in their career and life.

One of the things that I make time for during my week is to be a sounding board for students, new graduates, family, friends, and colleagues (current and past) who are trying to think through their career paths, career pivots, new job opportunities, or other career-related topics. I find it to be a very rewarding experience to help others think through their potential paths in life, from both a professional and personal standpoint.

ENGAGE A CAREER COACH

Throughout your career, there may be times when you might want to consider getting a career coach to help you think through things. This could be when you have taken on a new role or are considering a career transition and looking for some guidance. Either way, a career coach can be a helpful resource to tap into to help you think through things and define a path forward.

There is a range of career coaches in the world, and, depending on your company, there may be a network of coaches that you can tap into. I would also suggest asking for recommendations from colleagues and friends who have worked with a career coach, as this can be a good way to find the right one to fit your needs.

STRIVING FOR SUCCESS, THEN SIGNIFICANCE

About twenty years into my career, I attended an event where a woman was speaking about her career, and she shared this reflection...

"The first phase of your career is about success, and the second phase of your career is about significance."

This has stayed with me, and I reflect on it often these days, as I am definitely in the second phase of my career... and I continue to think about what it entails to achieve "significance." Obviously, the definition is going to vary by individual.

So, I am focused on achieving my definition of "significance" which is still being defined. This concept definitely motivates me when I reflect on how I am spending my time and what I choose to focus on each day in my career and in my life.

YOU ARE YOUR OWN CEO

It is important to remember there is no one else who can take control of your life and make it what you want it to be. You are in complete control.

This is a concept that was shared with me at some point during my career... and it really stuck with me... because it is so true.

There are times in our lives when we feel that we are not able to make the call that we want to make, whether it relates to a personal or professional decision. However, at the end of the day, we are the only ones who can make these decisions. It is up to each of us as individuals to think about how we want to design and structure our lives.

Once we embrace this concept, it can be very liberating as you think about the decisions you want to make about various aspects of your life.

CAREER REFLECTIONS FROM FRIENDS

As I was writing this book, I asked my friends to reflect on what they believe has made a difference in terms of how their children view their career. Here is what they shared...

"My kids understand that I work long hours and that hard work pays off. I hope this has given them an understanding of what kind of work ethic is required to be successful."

"Try not to let your kids see your stress. The balancing act will be stressful. But I never wanted my kids to know or see that, so they would not think it was their fault."

"Accept help... whether it is having another mom take your kid to sports practice or allowing your mother-in-law to take your daughter shopping. You literally can't do it all, so don't kill yourself trying. There will be opportunities to return the favors."

"Talk about work positively."

"Remind your children that you are not choosing work over them. Work is for you and for them."

"Keep the commitments. You cannot be everywhere, but you can give your children the time you promised and keep your work commitments, too."

"When my kids started asking questions about my work, I would answer their questions pretty directly and explain challenges, processes, mindsets, or successes. I think they can understand and appreciate more than we give them credit for, and it helps them develop an understanding about what I was/am doing while I am away from them. It models for them what work means. They also developed a sense of pride about what I did for work, which definitely felt good when I was dealing with guilt for putting them in daycare, etc."

"I talk to both my kids about the value of the work I do at home so they both value what stay-at-home and working moms do to make their homes run and their families thrive. I want my son to value all the work women do in the home and at a job outside the home. I also want my daughter to value all her future contributions to her family and her job and make sure she finds a partner who feels the same."

"I let them see the passion I have for what I do. I want them to know that I am not a one-dimensional person. I can be a loving mom and a nerdy, curious, competitive, driven physical therapist on a mission."

"I never talked about being a female in a predominantly male world. I just focused on being relentlessly prepared, delivering my results, and learning that not everything must be said. In the words of one of my co-workers, 'some things are better served cold' (versus in the heat of the moment)."

"I have found that my son's view of my career has evolved. There were times at younger ages when he felt like my work was taking time and attention away from him. As he has gotten older, he sees my passion for the work and appreciates not only that I am balancing both but sees how that success is important to me. My learning is that even though it is bumpy at times, stick with it, and do your best. Ultimately, your children see the importance and are proud of their parents who are doing their best."

BIGGEST SURPRISE FROM
THE JUGGLING ACT

The final question I asked my friends was, "What has been the biggest surprise you did not expect when you envisioned having a family and a career?"

"How hard and how fulfilling it can be, in equal measure."

"The realization that I needed the juggling act."

"How lonely I feel sometimes. It is really easy to get obsessed with work, kids, laundry, errands, sports, etc. I sometimes feel like I am fighting my own personal battle to keep it all going. It helps to connect with other working moms and talk, so that I know I'm not alone."

"That my traditional mother even turned around over time. When my son was born, she repeatedly asked when I was going to quit... 'You know, when you were young, I quit my job to stay home,' she would say to me. It was a soul-crushing comment... making me second-guess my choice to go back to work, but I stuck it out. When my son reached eighteen, heading off to college, I went through a divorce and was still working. She said, 'I am so glad you still have your career and kept working.' I am always surprised when my Mom changes her mind, as she is always right."

"Surprisingly, I got good at it over time. I learned how to release the small and unimportant things in both arenas, which meant that the concept of perfection and control went out the window."

My response to this question is...

"How much I loved the challenge of the juggling act... and can't imagine living my life any other way."

FAVORITE QUOTE FROM GRACE

One night at dinner, Grace and I were talking about my career, and she shared this reflection...

"I am so thankful you are a working mom.
We would have both gone crazy if you stayed at home."

Grace, Age 16

FAVORITE QUOTE

This is my favorite quote, which I have displayed on my desk in my home office... it makes me smile each time I read it.

"The master in the art of living
makes little distinction between
her work and her play,
her labor and her leisure,
her mind and her body,
her education and her recreation,
her love and her religion.
She hardly knows which is which.
She simply pursues her vision of excellence
in whatever she does, leaving others
to decide whether she is working or playing.
To her, she is always doing both."

James Michener

(Apologies to James Michener...
as I changed this quote from he/him to she/her)

TAKE A MOMENT
TO REFLECT...

CLOSING REFLECTIONS

When I started thinking about writing this book years ago, I was in the midst of trying to manage my own juggling act raising Grace. As I continued throughout my career, I would write down topics that I thought should be included in this book (if I ever decided to actually write it).

I am so happy to be sharing these reflections... and truly hoping that working parents who read this book can reflect on these bite-sized pieces of guidance to help them manage and enjoy their own juggling act.

So here's to the juggling act...

APPENDIX

NANNY INTERVIEW QUESTIONS

1) Why are you interested in being a nanny?

2) How long have you been a nanny?

3) Is childcare something you are doing temporarily, or do you intend to do it for a long time?

4) How old were the other children that you cared for?

5) What do you like about being a nanny?

6) What is your educational background?

7) Have you had any formal childcare training/childhood-development education?

8) Have you taken infant CPR and first-aid training? When was your most recent class?

9) What role does a good nanny play in a child's life?

10) How do you feel about caring for infants?

11) Describe how you might spend a typical day caring for and stimulating our child (mentally, physically, and emotionally).

12) How do you feel about structure and routine in a child's day-to-day life (versus allowing the child to define the schedule) in terms of eating, nap times, etc.?

13) Do you enjoy being outside (e.g., taking walks, going to the park, etc.)?

14) Are you able to swim? Do you enjoy the pool environment?

15) What do you do if a child is crying in their crib?

16) What do you think an infant needs most?

17) What do you think a toddler needs most?

18) When our child starts getting more active and "getting into things," how will you handle it?

19) How do you discipline young children?

20) What would you do if our child is sick or has an accident?

21) How do you comfort young children?

22) Please briefly walk through your work history, discussing your responsibilities and skills, and why you moved on from each position.

23) What are you looking for in a nanny situation?

24) How long do you envision staying with this position?

25) How do you feel about performing light housekeeping tasks (e.g., child's laundry, taking out trash, etc.) while the child is sleeping? Which tasks are you willing to do?

26) How comfortable are you with having a dog around you every day?

27) How do we communicate with you when you are not at work (text or email)?

28) Do you have your own car? What model/year?

29) Do you have children of your own?

30) Do you have any restrictions we should know about?

31) Do you smoke?

32) How many hours a week are you interested in working?

33) Would you be available to work evenings (overnight if necessary) or weekends (Saturday nights)?

34) What is your salary range (weekly)?

35) When could you start working?

36) Do you have any questions for us?

NANNY INTERVIEW SUMMARY

Date:	
Name:	
Mobile #:	
Home address:	
Own transportation/type:	
Hours available:	
Willingness for overnights:	
General availability:	
Availability to babysit on weekends:	
Salary requirements:	
Own children and ages:	
Smokes:	
Comfortable with dogs:	
Able to swim:	
Dietary restrictions:	
CPR training:	
Education/Childcare training:	

NANNY OVERVIEW

EXAMPLE GRACE – TWO YEARS OLD

Work Hours

- 8 a.m. – 6 p.m. (Monday–Friday), which equates to 50 hours per week

- Occasional babysitting on weeknights or weekends

- Occasional need for overnight stays when both parents are traveling

Compensation

- $XX per hour, which equates to $XX per week (paid weekly)

- $XX for overnight stays (6 p.m. – 8 a.m.)

- Taxes

- Paid Vacation: two weeks (ten weekdays per year)... please provide one month prior notice for any upcoming vacations.

- Paid Holidays: six days (Christmas Day, New Year's Day, Memorial Day, Fourth of July, Labor Day, Thanksgiving)

- Paid Sick/Personal Days: four days... please call by 7 a.m. on first day of illness.

- Notice for Leaving Position: please provide six weeks (at a minimum), but eight-plus weeks notice would be ideal.

Duties

- Feed breakfast/lunch/snacks.

- Give a bath in the morning... will also receive a bath at night if necessary.

- Dress for the day (any clothes in closet/dresser can be worn unless otherwise specified).

- Play with toys, read books, sing, dance, etc.... have fun!

- Visit with friends (see attached list).

- Take to Little Gym class (one day per week).

- Take to Music class (one day per week).

- Take to swimming lessons (during summer).

- Take to Park and Pool (in summer), Zoo, Botanical Garden, Center for Puppetry Arts, Science Museum, Bookstore for Reading Time, etc.... the more Grace experiences, the better!

- Keep a daily log of activities as well as eating and napping schedules.

- Please feel free to take pictures of Grace.

- Do Grace's laundry on Mondays and Fridays.

- Change Grace's bedding on Mondays.

- Empty Grace's trash on Mondays and Fridays.

- If time permits (and it does not take away from playing with Grace), please empty the dishwasher (if clean), take out the trash (if full), and vacuum family room (if needed).

- Please leave the house picked up and things put away at the end of the day.

- As necessary, Grace-related errands may be requested (e.g., returns to store or sending back via UPS).

Transportation

- Use own car with front-facing car seat.

- No talking on the cell phone while driving Grace in the car.

Parenting Philosophy

- Creating a fun, safe, learning environment is the priority on a day-to-day basis.

Naptime

- Grace is currently taking two naps a day.

- Mid-morning (around 10 a.m. for approximately one hour).

- Late afternoon (around 4 p.m. for approximately two hours).

Discipline

- Grace understands "No" and "No touch," and is aware of those items in the house she should not touch (e.g., TV, stereo equipment, remote, china cabinet in dining room, electrical outlets, toilets, etc.).

- If something should not be put in her mouth, Grace understands, "Do not put that in your mouth" or "Yuck."

- We are working on saying "Please."

Videos

- Grace is allowed to watch children's videos (e.g., Baby Einstein series, Veggie Tales, Disney).

Meals/Snacks

- Grace is allowed to eat food only in her highchair.

- Grace is allowed to drink from her sippy cup anywhere in the house (except for in bed).

- Grace is allowed to eat anything (except nuts, candy, and fast food, with the exception of pizza and Mexican).

- If she is not hungry, please do not force her to eat. She will motion with her hands when she is all done.

- Even after eating her meal (and motioning that she is all done), please offer her some fruit, which she will generally eat.

- Please give her milk and water at every meal. She drinks only milk or water at this point (in a sippy cup).

- Please have water out and available for her to drink at all times throughout the day.

- Snacks can be goldfish, raisins, fruit, crackers, graham crackers, etc.

- She must wear her bib while eating in her highchair. If she takes it off, then she is "done" eating.

- We are working on eating with a fork and/or a spoon.

Hygiene

- Please brush Grace's teeth in the morning after breakfast and in the evening prior to bed.

- Please wipe down the eating area in front of Grace's highchair with Windex or Fantastic after each meal/snack.

- Please wipe down Grace's highchair (if needed).

Safety

- Please watch Grace carefully on the stairs. Although she is confident in crawling up and down the stairs, she still does not have a sense of danger relative to the stairs.

- Please ensure Grace is buckled into the highchair.

- Please ensure Grace is buckled into the stroller, grocery cart, etc.

Emergencies

- If a medical emergency arises, please take Grace to the Emergency Room.

- Please contact us immediately

- Mom: (mobile #)

- Dad: (mobile #)

- Please contact Grace's pediatrician (office phone #)

BIRTHDAY QUESTIONS

1) What is your favorite color?
2) What is your favorite food?
3) What is your favorite lunch?
4) What is your favorite dinner?
5) What is your favorite dessert?
6) What is your favorite ice cream?
7) What is your favorite drink?
8) What is your favorite sport?
9) What is your favorite animal?
10) What is your favorite sea animal?
11) What is your favorite subject?
12) What is your favorite song?
13) What is your favorite book?
14) What is your favorite season?
15) What is your favorite flower?
16) What is your favorite tree?
17) What is your favorite piece of clothing?
18) What is your favorite place?
19) What do you want to be when you grow up?
20) Where do you want to live when you grow up?
21) What five places do you want to see in the world?
22) What is your favorite memory?
23) What is your special wish?

RECIPES

MUDBALLS

½ c. butter
4 c. crunchy peanut butter
1 lb. powdered sugar
3 c. Rice Krispies

Mix together and form into balls. Their size should be 1–2 bites, depending on your preference.

2 12-oz. bags of semisweet chocolate chips
1 stick paraffin (this is an edible wax which helps keep chocolate on the mudball)

In a small pan, melt ½ stick paraffin over low heat.

Once paraffin is fully melted, add chocolate chips.

Stir well, until chocolate chips are fully melted.

Keep the pan on low heat to ensure chocolate stays melted.

Place on wax paper to cool and set.

Once the full batch is complete, you can put mudballs in the refrigerator (not required).

Makes 80-100 mudballs per batch, depending on their size.

KNOX BLOCKS

3 small boxes of jello (any flavor)
3 envelopes of knox gelatin
4 c. boiling water

Stir well until dissolved.

Put into 9x12 pan to set.

Use cookie cutters to cut into shapes (e.g., hearts or stars).

CUTOUT COOKIES

4½ c. flour
½ tsp. salt
1 tsp. baking soda

Mix together.

1½ c. sugar
1¼ c. butter
1 tsp. vanilla extract
½ tsp. almond extract
3 eggs

Cream together.

Mix dry ingredients into butter-and-sugar mixture.

Roll out the dough with a rolling pin.

Cut shapes out of the dough.

Bake at 350°F for 8-10 minutes.

Makes 3 dozen cookies.

COOKIE FROSTING

1 c. confectioners sugar
1 egg white
3-4 drops lemon juice

Mix together.

Makes enough icing for 15-20 cookies.

THANKS
TO CONTRIBUTORS
REVIEWERS & SUPPORTERS

Just want to thank the contributors to this book...

Rebecca Messina, Stuart Kronauge, Andrea Fowler, Catharine Kelly, Sara Baker, and Lelia Dodson.

My special girlfriends who have each had your own working mom juggling act journeys and who spent time sharing your reflections based on your own experiences. Each of you helped to make the guidance in this book as universal as possible.

I also want to thank the reviewers of this book who took the time to read the book and provide insightful comments...

Beth Ames, Andrew Schulte, Ramin Baghai, Sally Ivester, Mia Graber, Alandha Scott, Rebecca Michael, Heather Boever, Marisa Tweed, and Candace Sabino.

I truly appreciate each of you taking the time (as you are in the midst of your own juggling acts) to share your reflections on which points resonated with you and where you wanted me to expand on a topic. This was incredibly helpful feedback as I worked to ensure this book was as comprehensive as possible.

I also want to thank everyone who has provided their encouragement and support throughout the process of writing this book. Most importantly, for all of the support each of you has given me over the years... you have been such an amazing part of my support network. I am so fortunate to have all of you in my life.

THANKS TO
MY BOOK TEAM

Thanks to Grace "Madden" Armstrong for editing my book. I loved collaborating with you during our working sessions. It was a very special experience to discuss details of this book with you and get your input to ensure that the guidance was as clear as possible and an accurate depiction of how I approached raising you. I will also never forget our negotiations about how many ellipses I could use in this book. My favorite moment is when you said, "Mom, just pick a punctuation... it can be a comma, a semi-colon, or a period... just pick something... no more ellipses!"

Thanks to Michele DeFilippo and Ronda Rawlins at 1106 Design for working with me on the editing process and book-cover design.

Thanks to Rachel Madden for helping me figure out the best font and color tone for my front cover.

Thanks to Bess Friday for taking the photo of the sculpture for the front cover. I also enjoyed collaborating with you as we worked to get the best shot possible for my back cover photo in my living room.

Thanks to Jon Krawczyk for being willing to collaborate with me to achieve my vision for the sculpture (on the front cover) in order to represent "The Juggling Act" quote.

Thanks to Katie Goellner for designing my book website.

Thanks to Gaye Carleton and Christi Cassidy at Mantra PR for their efforts in ensuring that the world knows this book is available to help working parents around the world with their juggling act.

SPECIAL THANKS

To my parents, Annette & Michael Madden... Thank you for being such amazing role models throughout my life. To my brothers and sisters-in-law... Dan & Tam Madden, and David & Rachel Madden... I am so fortunate to have such a loving and supportive family... you are all so special to me.

To my longtime boyfriend, Jack Selby... whom I lovingly refer to as "my diversion." Always loved our weekends together, which allowed me to unplug and recharge in order to manage the juggling act. The memories of our fun and relaxing times together will always make me smile. Importantly, thank you for pushing me to consider the possibilities as I was thinking through an important career decision and which path to follow. I will always remember you saying, "You owe it to yourself to consider it." You were right.

To my ex-husband, Rob Armstrong... I am proud of how we co-parented Grace together, both during our marriage and post-divorce. Truly appreciate that you have made it a priority to be the best Dad possible for Grace.

To my very special daughter, Grace "Madden" Armstrong... Thank you for being supportive of sharing our experiences to help others. I feel so fortunate to be your mom and have the opportunity to watch you learn about life and grow each year into the caring and giving person that you are to your family, friends, and community. It is so rewarding to see your wings flying and can't wait to see where they take you in life. I love you... xo Mom

JUGGLING ACT SCULPTURE STORY

After Grace graduated from high school, I decided to move from Atlanta to San Francisco. When I was working on the interior design for my new place, I was working with a designer to design a wall in the living room that would be a focal point.

As we were discussing the design elements of this wall, we considered adding a shelf running along the wall, and I wanted the shelf to be symmetrical on the wall. The designer said, "No, you should make it asymmetrical." Well, for those of you who don't know me... I am not really an asymmetrical type of girl, so I pushed back on this idea and said, "What am I going to do with that part of the shelf that is sticking out to the right?" The designer said, 'You can put a sculpture there."

I laughed and said with all that I had going on in terms of Grace graduating from high school, selling my house in Atlanta, moving my life across the country and buying/renovating/decorating this new place, and working full time, I really did not have time to figure out what type of sculpture would sit on this part of the shelf. This year was truly the biggest juggling act of my life.

So, over the months I started looking for sculptures online and could not find anything I liked.

One day I had a moment of inspiration and asked the woman I was working with to source art for my new place if she knew a metal sculptor. She said she knew one guy, but he would not be open to working with my ideas. Then she said, "I think

I actually know a sculptor in Malibu... and I think he would be willing to work with you."

So, she connected me with Jon Krawczyk. During my first discussion with Jon, he said, "Sarah, I do not have an ego, so you can tell me exactly what you want to create in this sculpture." I told Jon that this was good to hear because I had a very clear idea of what I wanted this sculpture to look like, and I wanted it to be on the front cover of the next book I was planning to finish writing in my new place. We collaborated over a couple of months and worked through the details together (from a distance). The result of our collaboration is the sculpture that you see on the front of this book.

As I mentioned earlier, this sculpture reflects the Juggling Act quote that I shared in the front of the book and the five balls we juggle in life... work, family, friends, health, and spirit.

When I moved to San Francisco, I was planning on finishing this book (which I had started on years before) once I was settled into my new place in San Francisco.

The sculpture now lives in my living room (and sits on the asymmetrical shelf). It was inspiration, as I wrote this book in my living room... and it makes me smile each time that I look at it.

BACKGROUND ON THE AUTHOR

Sarah Madden Armstrong was raised in Birmingham, Michigan, with two younger brothers and happily married parents (for more than fifty-five years and still going strong).

Sarah attended Georgetown University, as a scholarship athlete, earning a Bachelor of Science degree from the School of Business Administration with a major in Marketing. She was a four-year starter on the Georgetown University Volleyball Team.

Sarah began her career with Leo Burnett in Media. In 1997, she joined The Coca-Cola Company in Worldwide Media. In 2006, Sarah led the company's global approach to Agency Management. Her work has been recognized as industry-leading around the world, resulting in Sarah being named as one of *Ad Age's* "Women to Watch" and her inclusion in *Ad Age's Book of Tens* "Top Ten Who Made Their Mark." In 2017, Sarah joined McKinsey & Company, a leading global management consulting firm, as a Partner to advise clients around the world on agency management and marketing operations. In 2020, Sarah joined Google to lead Global Marketing Operations.

Sarah has a wanderlust for travel and has been fortunate to travel to 46 out of 50 states and 55+ countries so far. When she is not traveling, she is involved with Jack & Jill Late Stage Cancer Foundation and, over the years, has been involved with Georgetown Alumni Admissions Program and Trinity Table Soup Kitchen.

Sarah is also author of *The Mom's Guide to a Good Divorce* (which she self-published in 2016 through her publishing company Life Journey Experiences). Sarah does not think there is enough conversation in society about the concept of a "good divorce" and is hoping to help shift societal perception that a "good divorce" is an attainable outcome.

Sarah loves spending time with her daughter, Grace... whether it is exploring a new city, trying a new restaurant, listening to a new favorite playlist, watching a good movie, or entertaining friends... always enjoying the special moments together.

ALSO BY
SARAH ARMSTRONG

The Mom's Guide to a Good Divorce:

What to Think Through When Children Are Involved

Please pass this on to a working parent
who needs it...

or send them to thejugglingact.com

Printed in the USA
CPSIA information can be obtained
at www.ICGtesting.com
JSHW072230240724
66788JS00002B/2